Australian Curriculum

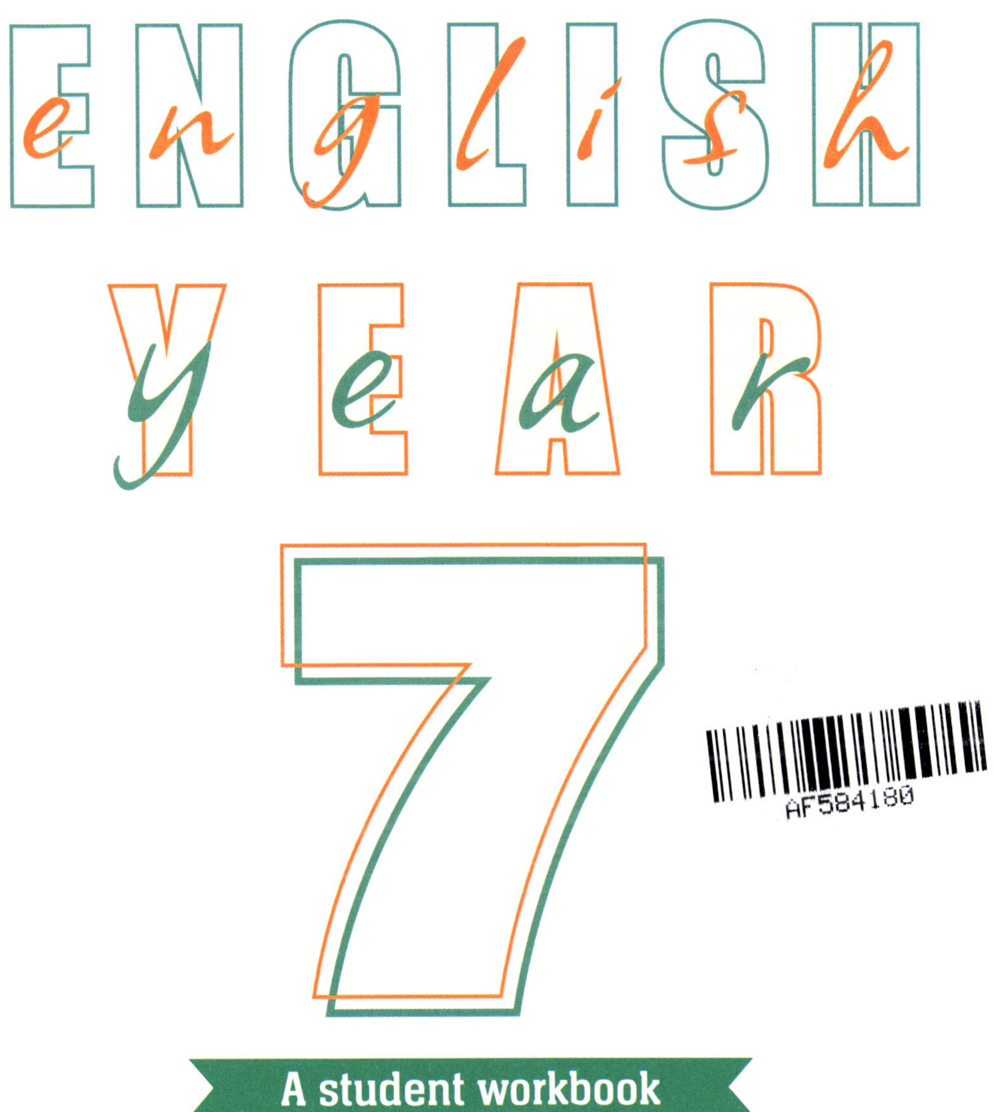

A student workbook

Leanne Bondin & Adam Kealley

Note to teachers

The *Australian Curriculum English* series is designed to assist student development of English skills, knowledge and understanding in interesting, engaging ways. The series aligns with Version 9.0 of the Australian Curriculum, ensuring that the Literature, Language and Literacy strands of the curriculum, as well as their sub-strands and threads, are seamlessly integrated and well balanced across the units of work. Each text in the series covers the entire curriculum content for its corresponding year level at least once, and in most instances several times, in order to highlight the varied approaches available to teachers and their students. Relevant Australian Curriculum content is specified in the introduction to each unit.

Each *Australian Curriculum English* book comprises 12 units, each of which is centred on a unifying theme, text type or significant English skill. Cumulatively, the units provide ample opportunity for students to practise their writing, reading, listening, speaking and viewing skills. The units can be completed in any order; teachers may find it useful to dip in and out of units in ways that complement their established teaching and learning programs.

The units include a number of text extracts, from familiar 'classics' to more contemporary and original texts. The extracts have been selected for their potential to illustrate particular curriculum content in action; teachers are encouraged to examine the texts independently to assess their suitability for their specific school context or cohort. While each unit includes multiple activities related to the unit focus, the final two units in the book closely target the specific comprehension strategies and grammar, punctuation and word knowledge specified in the Australian Curriculum English 7–10.

A range of colour-coded '**Check for understanding**' and '**Reflecting and discussing**' activities are embedded within the content of units 1–10. These activities are designed to:

- » help students strengthen and deepen their understanding of the concepts covered
- » encourage students to reflect carefully upon the content in relation to their own lives and experiences
- » facilitate meaningful whole-class or small-group interactions and discussion around the content.

Several '**Get creative**' activities within units 1–10 prompt students to create their own texts in a range of forms by practising writing, speaking and creating for different audiences and purposes. All activities make ideal classroom and/or homework tasks. Many of the written activities included can be completed within the fill-in lines provided.

As English teachers ourselves, we appreciate the importance of practical and helpful resources that supplement our own classroom practices and assist students to master essential curriculum content and skills. We sincerely hope that this series does just that for you and your students. To access suggested solutions to the activities in this workbook, please email us at: sales@insightpublications.com.au

Exploring ideas, events and issues

This unit examines the ways that ideas, events and issues can be identified and explored within a range of texts. By drawing on texts from varied contexts, including by First Nations authors and other wide-ranging Australian and world authors, you will learn how to identify ideas and express them clearly. This unit will also help you understand the techniques for elaborating, extending and explaining ideas through the use of complex and compound sentences.

In this unit you will learn:

- the difference between ideas, events and issues
- how to identify and explain ideas, events and issues
- to make connections between you, the world, and ideas, events and issues.

Curriculum content

Australian Curriculum content description	Content code
Understand how complex and compound-complex sentences can be used to elaborate, extend and explain ideas.	AC9E7LA05
Identify and explore ideas, points of view, characters, events and/or issues in literary texts, drawn from historical, social and/or cultural contexts, by First Nations Australian, and wide-ranging Australian and world authors.	AC9E7LE01

Identifying and exploring ideas

We all experience or encounter multiple ideas every day and we often share those ideas with each other. These may be as simple as a great idea for a weekend activity or as complex as an advanced concept like the theory of the Big Bang. So what *is* an idea exactly? Consider the following definitions:

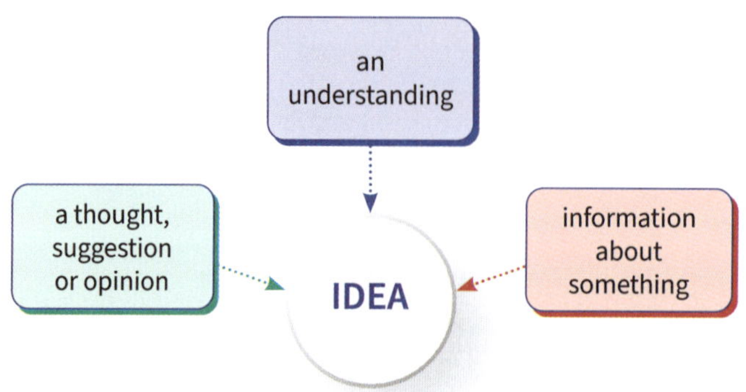

1.1 Reflecting and discussing

Discuss the following questions in pairs, in small groups or with the whole class, as directed by your teacher.

1. Look at the diagram above and pick the definition that best describes your understanding of an idea.
2. Research and discuss some additional definitions and **synonyms** for the word 'idea'.
3. Which of the following statements are ideas? Give reasons for your answers.
   a. I think I'll make a salad for dinner tonight.
   b. Dogs are better than cats.
   c. Our car ran out of petrol on the way home yesterday.
   d. Australia is both a continent and a country.
   e. Life would be better without social media.

synonym A word having nearly the same meaning as others (e.g. synonyms for 'old' include 'aged', 'venerable', 'antiquated')

Connecting themes to ideas

Ideas and themes are always present in the texts that we read, view or listen to. In fact, identifying the themes or ideas in a text is one of the first skills you learn in English and one that you will put into practice for the rest of your life. One of the easiest ways to identify ideas in a text is to think about its main themes and then to decide what the messages about those themes are.

Authors will not directly state what themes or ideas their texts are exploring. You have to draw your own conclusions based on the way the themes or ideas are presented *through* other aspects of the texts, such as plot events, characters and settings.

Some common themes in texts include the following:

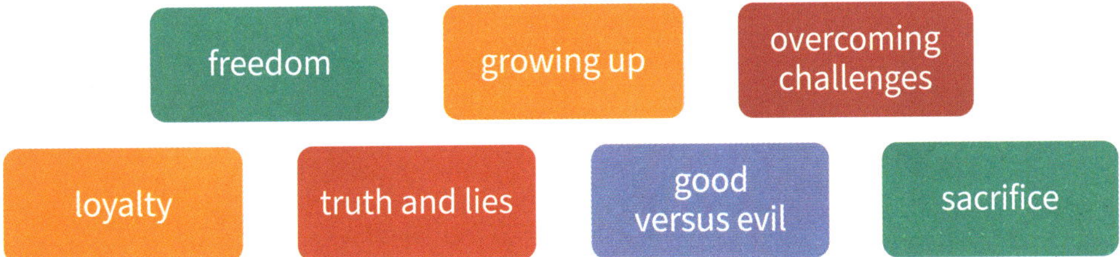

Expressing ideas and themes

While a theme is sometimes considered the main or 'big' idea of a text, themes should be expressed slightly differently to ideas. Read the following examples, which refer to imaginary texts.

Theme	Idea
The main theme of the film is *good versus evil.*	The film explores the idea that good will always triumph over evil.
Friendship is one of the main themes of the novel.	The novel emphasises the idea that true friendship is needed for people to feel happy.
The text includes the themes of *courage and loyalty.*	The idea that courage and loyalty were demanded of the soldiers is explored in the text.

You may notice that while themes can often be summarised in a few words or even in the form of abstract nouns such as 'love' or 'destiny', writing about ideas requires more elaboration. Ideas are best expressed within the context of a full sentence or main **clause**.

clause A grammatical unit referring to a happening or state e.g. 'the team won' (happening), 'the dog is red' (state), usually containing a subject and a verb group/phrase

1.2 Check for understanding

Decide whether the following are correct examples of ideas by adding them to the end of the sentence starter in the first column.

Sentence starter	Example	An idea? Y/N
The novel explores the idea that ...	young people feel lots of pressure to fit in with their peers.	
	peer pressure.	
	people who live below the poverty line are trapped in a vicious cycle.	
	Australia is a multicultural country.	
	multiculturalism.	

point of view The position from which the text is designed to be perceived (e.g. a narrator might take a role of first or third person, omniscient or restricted in knowledge of events or the opinion presented in a text)
perspective A lens through which the author perceives the world and creates a text, or the lens through which the reader or viewer perceives the world and understands a text
protagonist The main character in a text

Of course, you don't always need to include the word 'idea' within a sentence to identify an idea properly. For example, the sentence 'the poster suggests that girls and boys should be treated equally' naturally includes the idea that gender equality is being promoted.

Read the following extract from *Catch a Falling Star*, a novel by Western Australian author Meg McKinlay, and then answer the questions that follow. The extract is from a chapter titled 'Things That Fall From The Sky'. It is written in first-person narrative **point of view** from the **perspective** of a 12-year-old female **protagonist**, Frankie, who is an older sister to Newt.

Newt, once.

It was the middle of the night, pitch dark. He was halfway up a tree, trying to climb higher. I was standing at the bottom, trying to make him come down.

It was no one's fault.

It wasn't Mum's fault. She was exhausted from work and slept with earplugs so nothing but her alarm could wake her.

It wasn't Newt's fault. He was only four and there was no way he could understand.

It wasn't Kat's mum's fault. She was trying to be kind when she told Newt Dad was watching over him from above, that when he looked up at night, Dad would be the brightest star, shining down on him.

She couldn't have known Newt would take it literally. That he'd start climbing hills and ladders and rooftops in the middle of the night, trying to get as close as he could to the sky.

If it was anyone's fault, it was mine. I had hidden the ladder but I couldn't hide the trees. Maybe I should have told Mum. I always meant to. I'd lead Newt back to the house, tuck him in, and plan to tell her tomorrow.

But when morning came, I never did. Mum always seemed like she had enough to worry about already, with working all the time and those envelopes that kept arriving with red writing saying "Overdue" and "Final reminder".

So I didn't say anything – not to Mum and not to Newt. I didn't tell him Dad wasn't really a star. I didn't want to be the one to take that away from him. Instead, I started sleeping with my door open, listening for his footsteps in the hall.

That night, I didn't hear him until he was on the verandah. By then, it was too late to stop him climbing. All I could do was try to talk him back down.

When he fell, I caught him. Or at least, I broke his fall. He had the wind knocked out of him – and so did I – but he didn't break anything. He was okay. We both were. And so we could go back to bed, wake up in the morning, and pretend it was all a dream.

1.3 Check for understanding

1 Select which ideas are communicated in the extract from the following options. There may be more than one correct answer.

a Frankie feels responsible for looking after her younger brother. ☐

b Frankie and Newt's father is always at work. ☐

c Newt is afraid of heights. ☐

d Frankie and Newt's father has passed away. ☐

e Frankie feels protective of both her mother and her brother. ☐

2 Find a sentence in the extract that supports one of the ideas communicated in the extract.

___

___

3 Select one of the ideas from the list above and explain how it is/is not relatable to your own experiences. For example, do you also share a sense of responsibility or protectiveness for others?

___

___

___

Elaborating, extending and explaining ideas

In English, you will usually be required to fully explain the ideas explored within texts by elaborating and extending your discussion of them. This can be achieved in lots of ways, including through verbal explanation, through analytical writing, or even in visual form within mind maps or diagrams.

One of the ways in which ideas can be elaborated, extended or explained is through using a variety of sentence structures with an understanding of how clauses work.

A clause is a group of words that includes a subject and a verb:

for example, 'the dog barked'.

It is important to understand the three main sentence structures, each of which contains different combinations of clauses. They are:

- **simple sentences**
- **compound sentences**
- **complex sentences.**

Read the following definitions and examples of these three different sentence structures.

Sentences	Explanation	Example
Simple	Simple sentences contain one clause. They express one idea.	Shakespeare's plays are still relevant.
Compound	Compound sentences contain two or more linked main clauses joined by a **conjunction** (e.g. but, and). Additional clauses can add more information or additional ideas.	Shakespeare's plays are still relevant and people enjoy their entertaining characters.
Complex	Complex sentences consist of a main clause and a subordinate clause that provides more information. The subordinate clause will not make sense on its own.	Shakespeare's plays are still relevant, mostly because their entertaining characters highlight complex human emotions and relationships.

conjunction In a sentence, a word that joins other words, groups/phrases or clauses together in a logical relationship such as addition, time, cause or comparison. There are 2 types: coordinating and subordinating

While some ideas explored in texts can be expressed in simple sentences, complex and compound sentences can be used to elaborate, extend and explain them in more detail. Read the following example based on the historical non-fiction text, *Sadako and the Thousand Paper Cranes,* written by Eleanor Coerr and published in 1977. Each sentence contains at least one idea.

Simple sentence → Sadako is a very determined person.

Complex sentence → Sadako demonstrates determination by making 1,000 paper cranes in order to be granted a wish, despite being gravely ill with leukaemia due to exposure to the atomic bomb that hit her Japanese home town of Hiroshima in 1945.

Compound sentence → Her determination is an inspiring quality, and it has encouraged many people who face their own challenges.

1.4 Check for understanding

Choose a text you have read or viewed. Following the model above, write your own short paragraph that uses a combination of simple, compound and complex sentences to express an idea explored in your chosen text. Label each type of sentence structure in the margins as in the example above.

____

____

____

____

____

1.5 Get creative

1 It can be difficult to come up with good story ideas for your own creative writing. Try using the following approach to develop an idea for the plot of a narrative by mixing and matching one selection from each of the three columns below. Highlight one element in each column.

Main character/s	Main setting	Important object to feature
teenage girl	kitchen	diamond ring
old man	school classroom	shoe
identical twins	train carriage	television remote
talking dog	deserted island	pencil
lost child	graveyard	book

2 Plan an idea for a short story plot that connects all three elements you highlighted.

3 Draft and **edit** your short story.

Identifying and exploring events

The made-up events that unfold within a fiction text are referred to as the plot. The events – or plot – make up the main storyline and interest points of any novel, short story, film, drama script or other fiction text. The order in which those events unfold within the story is its **narrative** structure. To identify the events in a text, you simply need to ask yourself, 'What happens in the text?' For example, the early events in the well-known book *Harry Potter and the Philosopher's Stone* by J. K. Rowling include the following.

edit To prepare, alter, adapt or refine with attention to grammar, spelling, punctuation and vocabulary

narrative The selection and sequencing of events or experiences, real or imagined, to tell a story to entertain, engage, inform and extend imagination, typically using an orientation, complication and resolution

» Harry is orphaned and must live with his cruel aunt, uncle and cousin.

» Harry receives a letter stating he will go to Hogwarts School of Witchcraft and Wizardry.

» Harry arrives at Hogwarts.

Non-fiction texts, such as autobiographies, feature articles and persuasive speeches, frequently respond to or explore *real* events. Read the following extract from the first chapter of *Young Dark Emu: A Truer History* by Bruce Pascoe, a Yuin, Bunurong and Tasmanian man born in Melbourne.

Once their sentence had been served, many convicts chose to remain in the colony and acquire land. Owning land was something they could never have done if they had returned to England.

In the new colony, administrators and soldiers made themselves rich by buying and selling land. When free settlers began to arrive, they too were greedy for land and quickly acquired any that was available. With all available government land allocated, the newcomers turned to outlying districts beyond the ranges and coves of Sydney. They took with them plenty of weapons and men to use them.

In the earliest days of the colony, Aboriginal people tried to draw the British into the codes of behaviour they expected from 'visitors'. But the colonisers had no intention of respecting Aboriginal law and wholesale war broke out.

The colonisers forcibly drove Aboriginal people from the land, killing thousands in the process in fierce and bloody battles. Aboriginal people could not fall back into neighbouring lands as they had been born to live on, and protect, only the land of their birth – their Country. Once defeated, the Aboriginal people remained within their old clan boundaries, but there they were at the mercy of the colonists who had stolen their land. Initially Aboriginal people fought back. There is evidence of battles across the continent including on the plains near Robinvale on the Murray River, on the Crawford River in western Victoria, Oyster Bay in Tasmania, Geraldton in Western Australia, the Pascoe River in Queensland, the Hawkesbury in New South Wales and thousands of other locations.

1.6 Check for understanding

1 Provide definitions or explanations for the following words from the extract.

a colonisers ______________________________

b acquire ______________________________

c codes of behaviour ______________________________

d wholesale ______________________________

e clan ______________________________

2 Compile a summarised list of the events that are retold in the extract above. Try to list them in the same order in which the author presents them.

____

____

3 Why do you think the subtitle of this book is 'A Truer History'?

Identifying and exploring issues

Issues can be defined as topics of concern that cause differences of opinion. Many of the texts that you study in English will explore global, national or local issues. Both fiction and non-fiction texts can explore issues. This means that their authors have focused on aspects of society that provoke different opinions, conversations or debates. Some examples of current issues are:

- the minimum age of criminal responsibility
- cyber bullying
- climate change
- gender discrimination
- the treatment of asylum seekers and refugees.

1.7 Reflecting and discussing

Discuss the following questions in pairs, in small groups or with the whole class, as directed by your teacher.

1 What is meant by each of the topics listed above? You may need to conduct some additional research.

2 What different opinions might people have on these issues? Who do you think is most likely to have these different opinions?

3 Brainstorm a list of other issues that cause debate and different opinions in society.

An exploration of issues in texts allows us to understand the world and people around us. Consider some of the issues explored in the following texts.

Issues explored:

» racism
» financial abuse
» sexism
» mental health.

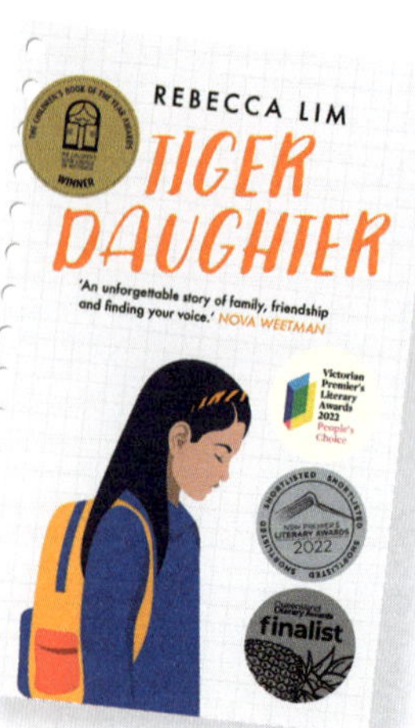

Issues explored:

» climate change
» sustainability
» poverty/economic disadvantage.

1.8 Get creative

1 Choose a novel or film you have read or viewed. Following the examples above, brainstorm a list of at least three issues explored in your chosen novel or film.

___

___

___

2 Now design a new cover or promotional poster for the text you have read or viewed. Aim to visually represent one or more of the issues it explores. You might like to use an online program for this task.

Non-fiction texts also frequently explore issues. The following extract is from the *Kids News* website. Read it carefully, thinking about the main issue it explores.

Scan the QR code, or click here to access the extract.

Animated film study: Up

This unit invites you to explore the magical worlds of animated films. The focus will be on identifying and explaining the ways that characters, settings and events combine to create meaning. You will be helped to form and justify opinions, and to compare and share these opinions with others. This unit will also assist you to understand the techniques used to construct multimodal texts such as animated films, as well as to understand their purpose. The 2009 animated film *Up* (especially the first 12 minutes) will be used as a case study to help illustrate some of these concepts.

In this unit you will learn:

- about the multimodal features of animated films
- to form an opinion about characters, setting and events in animated film texts
- how to evaluate animated film texts in the form of a film review.

Curriculum content

Australian Curriculum content description	Content code
Recognise language used to evaluate texts including visual and multimodal texts, and how evaluations of a text can be substantiated by reference to the text and other sources.	AC9E7LA02
Identify and describe how texts are structured differently depending on their purpose and how language features vary in texts.	AC9E7LA03
Analyse how techniques such as vectors, angle and/or social distance in visual texts can be used to create a perspective.	AC9E7LA07
Form an opinion about characters, settings and events in texts, identifying areas of agreement and difference with others' opinions and justifying a response.	AC9E7LE02
Identify and explain the ways that characters, settings and events combine to create meaning in narratives.	AC9E7LE05
Plan, create, rehearse and deliver presentations for purposes and audiences in ways that may be imaginative, reflective, informative, persuasive and/or analytical, by selecting text structures, language features, literary devices and visual features, and using features of voice including volume, tone, pitch and pace.	AC9E7LY07

Understanding multimodal texts

multimodal A combination of 2 or more communication modes (e.g. print, image and spoken text, as in film or computer presentations)
mode Various processes of communication – listening, speaking, reading or viewing and writing or creating

Have a look at the film poster. Did you notice that it combines writing and visual images? This makes it a **multimodal** text. Films typically use multiple (two or more) **modes** of communication and therefore they are also multimodal texts.

The modes of communication in animated films involve us in listening and viewing – and sometimes reading – all at the same time. The multiple modes usually work together to create meaning.

Think about the last animated film you watched. Chances are it included the following elements:

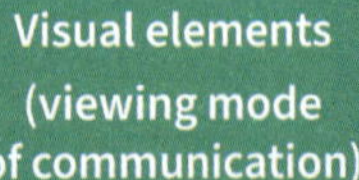

Elements	Examples
Visual elements (viewing mode of communication)	» camera angles » shot types » colour
auditory/aural elements (listening and speaking modes of communication)	» spoken dialogue » background music » sound effects
Written elements (reading mode of communication)	» credits » captions » signs

2.1 Check for understanding

Decide whether the following features of multimodal texts are examples of visual, auditory or written modes of communication by rewriting them underneath the correct heading in the table below.

clothing	facial expression	music	speech/dialogue
colour	lighting	close-up shot	sound effects
credits	body language	captions	voice-over

Visual	Auditory (sometimes referred to as 'aural')	Written
List features you look at or see below	List features you hear or listen to below	List features you read in written form below

What is an animated film?

Animation is the process of bringing illustrations or objects to life through motion pictures so that they seem to be moving. Animation remains one of the most time-consuming and complex of all **cinematographic** techniques. Disney, Pixar and DreamWorks have all become well known for producing animated films.

cinematography The science and art of shooting motion-picture scenes, including the camera work and lighting

Stop-motion is a kind of animation technique which involves the camera being constantly stopped and started again between each frame to record the tiny movements of objects, such as plasticine or puppets. *Coraline* and *Fantastic Mr. Fox* are examples of stop-motion animation.

2.2 Reflecting and discussing

Discuss the following questions in pairs, in small groups or with the whole class, as directed by your teacher.

1 What animated films have you seen?

2 What is your favourite animated film? Provide reasons.

3 How are animated films similar to or different from other feature films?

Creating a perspective

Visual features can work to create a **perspective** – a lens through which the viewer or **audience** sees the world within the film. Search online for a high camera angle image. The perspective created may be one where we viewers see the character as small and vulnerable because we are looking down on them. We might understand the character as disempowered in the world of the film, at least in the moment captured by this camera angle.

perspective A lens through which the author perceives the world and creates a text, or the lens through which the reader or viewer perceives the world and understands a text

audience An intended or assumed group of readers, listeners or viewers that a writer, designer, filmmaker or speaker is addressing

2.3 Check for understanding

1 Apart from films, what other types of texts are multimodal due to their combination of written, visual and/or auditory/aural features?

____

____

____

2 Provide definitions for the following words. Use a dictionary if necessary, but make sure the definitions relate to visual language.

a gaze ______

b framing ______

c vectors ______

d composition ______

e mise en scène ______

Exploring characterisation

Many animated films are narratives; that is, they tell a story. They therefore contain the **conventions** or ingredients of any good tale. These conventions include characters, settings and plot events.

convention An accepted practice that has developed over time and is generally used and understood (e.g. use of punctuation)

Most animated films contain one or two main characters. The main character/s will be faced with a problem or difficulty that they must overcome. Many times, this challenge will take the form of a journey.

Here are some examples.

- Nemo's father must negotiate all kinds of dangerous obstacles to find his missing son in *Finding Nemo*.
- In *The Good Dinosaur,* Arlo must travel a great distance through harsh conditions to be reunited with his family after he is separated from them during a storm.
- Moana, in the film of the same name, must navigate a dangerous, action-packed voyage over the ocean in order to save her people.

protagonist The main character in a text

This familiar plotline of a main character – the **protagonist** – embarking on a difficult quest or voyage is sometimes referred to as the 'hero's journey'.

One unlikely hero in an animated film is Carl Fredricksen from the 2009 Disney–Pixar film *Up*, directed by Pete Docter and Bob Peterson.

The film tells the story of Carl, a cranky old man, who ties thousands of balloons to his house and attempts to float all the way to the South American wilderness after his wife passes away. Little does he know that a young boy called Russell is a stowaway in his balloon-powered house. Together, they encounter lots of complications as they try to reach Paradise Falls, Carl's dream destination.

Characters are developed using a range of techniques such as their dialogue, actions, appearance, and interactions or relationships with others. These characterisation techniques tell us about the kind of people they are.

2.4

Check for understanding

Watch the first seven minutes of *Up* (to the end of the childhood scenes). Concentrate on the characterisation of Carl Fredricksen as a young boy, filling out the table with examples from the film.

Character: Carl Fredricksen			
Dialogue (speech)	**Actions**	**Appearance**	**Relationships with others**

Now answer the following questions in the spaces provided.

1 Explain you first impression of Carl. How would you best describe his personality and the type of person he is?

____

____

2 Ellie says to Carl, 'I ripped this right out of a library book!' What does this dialogue show about Ellie's personality? Consider how she is characterised as someone who is different from Carl.

____

____

3 **Values** are individual principles or ideals that a person believes in. Circle the values below that you think are most important to Carl as a young boy.

education	adventure	financial wealth
family	friendship	exploration

values Ideas and beliefs specific to individuals and groups

The characters in animated films are visually designed to reflect aspects of their personality. Their facial and physical features, as well as their clothing, accessories and mannerisms, often tell us a great deal about what sort of people they are.

Exploring setting

A setting is the time and place where the action of a story takes place. Settings are important because they often impact on the characters or affect the plot in meaningful ways. Settings of place can be as specific as a character's bedroom or as broad as the country in which they live. Time settings can equally be narrowed to a particular date or left as open as an unspecified time 'in the future'.

mise en scène In film, the composition of a shot, including elements such as lighting, costumes, props, set design and special effects

Settings are displayed in films through **mise en scène**. The term 'mise en scène' includes everything that is captured by the camera, such as costumes, lighting, props and locations. These features reveal something about the scene and help to create a mood.

2.5 Check for understanding

Reflect on the first seven minutes of *Up,* and then answer the following.

1 Tick three clues that tell the audience that the opening of the film is set in the past.

a Carl goes to the movies. ☐

b The movie Carl watches is in black and white. ☐

c Carl imagines he is an explorer. ☐

d The narrator uses language such as 'golly' and 'the bee's knees'. ☐

e Carl is wearing old-fashioned flying goggles. ☐

2 Think about the following ideas for a story and provide suggestions about what settings would be appropriate for each of them. Some possible settings to choose from are provided below the story ideas.

a A girl is picked on by her classmates because of her scruffy uniform. ________

b An alien race decides to unite and take control of Earth. ________

c A young man quits his boring job to pursue a life as an actor. ________

Possible settings: Mars, a city office, a school classroom.

3 List some of the ways in which a film director might tell the audience about where a story is set.

____

____

Exploring events

The events that unfold in an animated film are what hold our attention and keep us interested enough to keep watching until the end. The events in a **narrative** usually happen in a particular order, beginning with an introduction to some kind of problem or complication to be overcome by the characters. This part of the story is called the orientation or exposition. The events that follow build towards an exciting climax – the part of the film you really don't want to miss! The climax usually happens close to the end of the film. The final events offer some sort of resolution where you learn how the conflict or problem has been resolved.

narrative The selection and sequencing of events or experiences, real or imagined, to tell a story to entertain, engage, inform and extend imagination, typically using an orientation, complication and resolution

The relationship between characterisation, setting and events

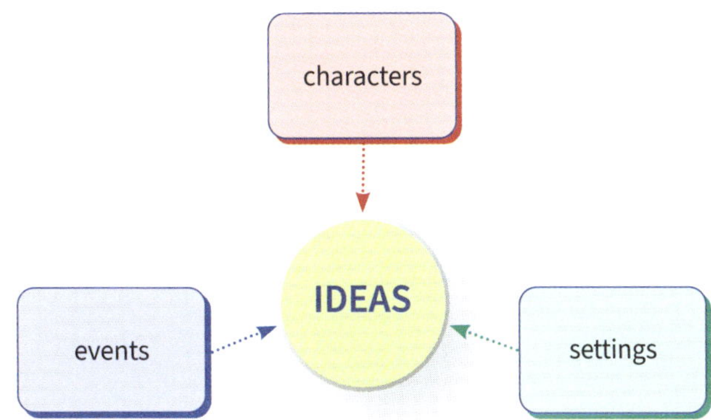

Characterisation, setting and events all work *together* to create meaning in an animated film. The meaning created by the characters, setting and events can include its main ideas, themes and messages.

For example: The idea that Carl in *Up* wants to honour his wife's memory is conveyed by his determination to reach Paradise Falls and his resilience in dealing with many disruptive events along the way, such as Russell being trapped in his house.

Observe how all of these aspects – characterisation, setting and events – relate to each other and contribute to the ideas that are communicated. Without any one of them, the meaning of the film would be unclear.

Considering purpose

Animated films fulfil a range of **purposes** or reasons for being made. Common purposes include:

» to entertain audiences

» to make money for the production company

» to experiment with new ways of filmmaking.

purpose An intended or assumed reason for a type of text

theme The main idea, concept or message of a text

Animated films often explore very serious and mature **themes** or ideas. Therefore, the purpose of texts like these can also be to explore issues and teach us all important lessons.

2.6 Check for understanding

The following table is a record of some popular animated films that examine serious themes and teach us important messages. In groups or as a class, complete the table below. You may need to do some research if you are unfamiliar with some of these films.

Film	Purpose: to present the following messages, lessons or ideas
Mulan	› Gender stereotypes are dangerous and should challenged. › Women can be just as capable as men.
Encanto	
Moana	
Frozen	
Beauty and the Beast	
Inside Out	

Emotions and opinions

Like most animated films, *Up* is not just about lighthearted, happy subjects such as adventure and friendship. In fact, there are some serious themes explored in the film too; such as loss, ageing and loneliness. Emotions are the feelings we experience, usually in reaction to something that we see or that happens to us. Some common emotions include:

joy | excitement | happiness | confusion | anger | fear | sadness | despair

There are some emotional scenes explored in *Up* related to loss, ageing and loneliness. Watch the scenes showing the relationship between Carl and Ellie from 0:07:13 to 0:11:30.

2.7 Reflecting and discussing

Discuss the following questions in pairs, in small groups or with the whole class, as directed by your teacher.

1 What emotions do you feel as you watch these scenes?

2 There is no speaking (dialogue) in this sequence of scenes. What is the effect and impact of this?

Not only do we feel emotional responses to the films that we watch, but we can also develop opinions about them. Opinions are individual judgements that we make about something, rather than facts about them. They are based on our personal feelings and tastes.

Film review language

In English, you will be encouraged to talk about and share your personal opinions with others. It doesn't matter if others agree or disagree with your opinion, but it is important that you explain *why* you reached that opinion. You might develop a positive or negative opinion of an animated film for some of the following reasons, but there are plenty of others too.

» The characters were/were not relatable and believable.

» The film's animation effects were/were not very effective and cleverly executed.

» The storyline was/was not exciting and original.

One way in which personal opinions can be shared with others is through reviews. Written reviews of films and books appear on websites or in magazines and newspapers, online or in print. They include evaluative words and statements – language used to express a judgement or opinion about a topic. **Evaluative language** can include **adjectives**, **adverbs** and comparisons.

evaluative language Positive or negative language that judges the worth of something. It includes language to express feelings and opinions; make judgements; and assess quality of objects, ideas and features of texts

adjective A word class that describes, identifies or quantifies a noun or a pronoun, e.g. two (number or quantity), my (possessive), ancient (descriptive), shorter (comparative), wooden (classifying)

adverb A word class that may modify a verb (e.g. 'softly' in 'the boy sings softly'), an adjective (e.g. 'really' in 'he is really strong') or another adverb (e.g. 'very' in 'the toddler walks very slowly')

2.8

Check for understanding

1 The following evaluative words or statements might be included in a film review. Decide whether they demonstrate a positive or negative judgement and place them in the correct columns in the table below.

confusing	impressive	disappointing	highly entertaining
an absolute must-see	the best yet	uninspired	poorly executed
visually spectacular	a time-waster	repetitive	

Positive	Negative

2 Plan and create your own film review on a film you have seen recently or another that you remember from your childhood. It may be a negative or a positive review.

____

____

____

____

3 Rehearse and then deliver a brief oral presentation to accompany your film review in small groups or to the whole class. You will want to make sure you draw on persuasive and evaluative language features and techniques with the language that you use. Consider also the importance of volume, tone, pitch and pace when delivering your presentation.

Understanding persuasive texts

From social media advertisements that encourage us to buy a product, to friends convincing us to stay up all night during a sleepover, to people encouraging us to agree with their opinions on television shows, persuasive appeals are everywhere. This unit will help you understand how persuasive texts, such as speeches, essays and advertisements, are constructed using language and structural features that match their persuasive purpose and the audience they want to convince.

In this unit you will learn:

- about persuasive language features, text structures and organisation
- how to identify the purpose and audience of a persuasive text.

Curriculum content

Australian Curriculum content description	Content code
Recognise language used to evaluate texts including visual and multimodal texts, and how evaluations of a text can be substantiated by reference to the text and other sources.	AC9E7LA02
Identify and describe how texts are structured differently depending on their purpose and how language features vary in texts.	AC9E7LA03
Understand that the cohesion of texts relies on devices that signal structure and guide readers, such as overviews and initial and concluding paragraphs.	AC9E7LA04
Investigate the role of vocabulary in building specialist and technical knowledge, including terms that have both everyday and technical meanings.	AC9E7LA08
Use interaction skills when discussing and presenting ideas and information including evaluations of the features of spoken texts.	AC9E7LY02
Explain the structure of ideas such as the use of taxonomies, cause and effect, extended metaphors and chronology.	AC9E7LY04

Persuasive language features and techniques

language features Features that support meaning (e.g. clause- and word-level grammar, vocabulary, figurative language, punctuation, images). Choices vary for the purpose, subject matter, audience and mode or medium
audience An intended or assumed group of readers, listeners or viewers that a writer, designer, filmmaker or speaker is addressing

Persuasive texts include certain types of **language features** and techniques that work to convince an **audience**. Some common persuasive language features are listed in the table below. Some examples provided are from the famous 1963 'I Have a Dream' speech by Dr Martin Luther King, Jr.

Language feature	Definition	Example
rhetorical question	a question that is asked to make people think and not to receive an answer	'Don't you want freedom and justice?'
alliteration	repeating the same consonant sound at the beginning of words that are close together	'<u>s</u>ongs of <u>s</u>alvation to <u>s</u>alve the <u>s</u>oul'
emotive language	deliberately strong words that provoke an emotional response	'great beacon light of hope', 'withering injustice'
inclusive language	words to make an audience feel included, such as 'we', 'our' or 'us'	'foundations of <u>our</u> nation', 'when <u>we</u> allow freedom'
repetition	repeating words, phrases or ideas for emphasis	The line 'I have a dream' is used <u>eight times</u> in the speech.
high-modality language	words or phrases with a high degree of certainty, such as 'must', 'definitely', 'certainly' and 'without a doubt'	'As we walk, we <u>must</u> make the pledge that we <u>shall</u> always march ahead.'
direct address	directly addressing the audience with the pronoun 'you'	'Let us not wallow in the valley of despair, I say to <u>you</u> today, my friends.'

Persuasive techniques and evidence

Persuasive texts can use a range of techniques involving evidence to convince their audiences. These techniques take many forms, such as the following types of evidence:

- *statistics:* number facts that tell us something about a group of people or a set of data
- *facts:* pieces of information that can be proved to be true
- *expert opinions:* statements or information from people or organisations considered to be experts on a particular subject
- *personal anecdotes:* short stories and reflections based on personal experience
- *case studies:* research studies or practical examples taken from the real world.

Persuasive text structures and organisation

Written and spoken persuasive texts can be structured and organised in a variety of ways. Some of the most common sequences are listed below.

Beginning	Middle	Ending
› an introduction to the topic with a clear statement of the opinion or contention that the audience is being persuaded to agree with › an overview of different viewpoints on the topic › an anecdote that illustrates the topic or issue › a rhetorical question or a series of rhetorical questions	› 3–4 main points around which separate body paragraphs are developed › evidence and examples used to support points, such as statistics, case studies, facts, expert opinions, anecdotes and analogies	› a clear conclusion that summarises the main points and reiterates the main contention › a return to the beginning by reflecting on the topic or revisiting an opening anecdote › a proposed solution or a call to action

3.1 Check for understanding

Find definitions for the following terms.

1 contention ______________________________

2 anecdote ______________________________

3 analogy ______________________________

4 call to action ______________________________

Other structural elements you might find in persuasive texts include:

taxonomy

A way of classifying or organising things. Usually, the most important thing is placed first, as in a hierarchy. In planning a persuasive text, you might list all your ideas in a visual taxonomy first, from best idea to weakest, and then include only the top three.

cause and effect

A technique where an action or event is outlined, and then the outcome or result of that action or event is expressed. For example, a persuasive essay may argue that because fast food is too cheap and available, obesity rates are increasing.

extended metaphor

A single **metaphor** or analogy that stretches over multiple lines or even a whole text. For example, a persuasive speech may present racism as a dangerous, deadly virus at different points throughout the speech.

metaphor A type of figurative language used to describe a person or object through an implicit comparison to something with similar characteristics

Persuasive essays

Like analytical essays, persuasive essays are typically structured with an introduction, a number of body paragraphs and a conclusion. They attempt to persuade the reader of a particular opinion. They need to include evidence to support their argument.

Observe the following essay structure.

Introduction	State your contention (your opinion). Give three reasons for your opinion.
Body paragraphs **(TEEL structure)** **Repeat this sequence for all body paragraphs**	T = topic sentence. The first sentence should explain what the paragraph will be about. E = evidence and examples. Give examples and evidence that support the main point you are making in the paragraph. Evidence can include statistics, facts, expert opinions, personal anecdotes and case studies. E = explanation. Explain how this evidence or these examples prove your point. L = link to topic. Relate your point back to the topic of your essay. This will help your essay to stay on track.
Conclusion	Wrap up your argument and restate your contention using different words.

Read the following example of an introduction and first body paragraph which respond to this topic: '*Growing up is a positive experience.* Write a persuasive essay in response to this statement'.

Introduction states contention and three reasons for it.	Growing up is undoubtedly a positive experience. This is because we gain more rights and we become more knowledgeable and skilled as we mature. We also become more capable of deciding how we want to live our lives. These benefits outweigh the small number of negative changes experienced while growing up.
Topic sentence outlines what the paragraph will be about. **Evidence and examples** support the point. **Explain** why the evidence proves the point. Final sentence **links** back to the topic.	As we age, we gain new rights that we didn't have before. This means that we get to have a say in how our country is run and over important matters such as the economy, education and health care. For instance, when we are eighteen, we can vote. The right to vote, along with the right to drive a car, get a job and drink alcohol, are examples of rights we only get when we reach adulthood. 88% of new voters surveyed by the Australian Government reported feeling more independent when they gained this right. Rights like these positively affect our daily lives and those of our families and friends. These are all major developments in an individual's life, meaning that growing up results in more positive changes than negative ones.

3.2 Get creative

The example essay only provides one body paragraph, which argues the first point: that 'we gain more rights as we grow up'. The ideas for paragraphs two and three are as follows:

- We become more knowledgeable and skilled as we grow up.
- We become more capable of deciding how we want to live our lives as we mature.

Following the TEEL paragraph structure outlined previously, write your own second *or* third paragraph for the essay.

Topic sentence:

____

____

Evidence and examples:

____

____

____

Explanation:

____

____

____

Linking sentence:

____

____

Sometimes, a persuasive essay might offer a counterargument in another body paragraph just before the conclusion. Sometimes this is done because acknowledging and then immediately refuting a counterargument can provide more persuasive impact. A counterargument is one that opposes the main contention.

Can you think of a counterargument for the essay topic above? Why do you think growing up might *not* be a positive experience?

Creating cohesion

Cohesion is about creating unity within a text so that all of its parts are connected. In persuasive texts, one way to create cohesion is to use **connectives** to signal a transition between points, sentences or paragraphs.

cohesion Grammatical or lexical relationships that bind different parts of a text together and give it unity. It is achieved through devices such as reference, substitution, repetition and text connectives

connective Words linking, and logically relating ideas to one another, in paragraphs and sentences indicating relationships of time, cause and effect, comparison, addition, condition and concession or clarification

3.3

Check for understanding

1 Sort the following connectives into the columns of the table where they best fit.

secondly furthermore finally moreover
additionally in summary lastly firstly

Near the beginning of a persuasive text (e.g. first body paragraph)	At the introduction of a new point, sentence or paragraph	Near the end of a persuasive text (e.g. last body paragraph or conclusion)

2 Add suitable connectives to your TEEL paragraph above in order to improve its cohesion.

Persuasive speeches

Persuasive speeches are some of the most common types of persuasive text. They can be delivered and listened to in a wide range of situations, such as at protest rallies, during debates, within sales pitches and in courtrooms.

3.4

Check for understanding

When Deng Thiak Adut was six years old, he was taken away from his family farm in South Sudan and forced to join an army before being smuggled out of the country with the help of his brother. Read the edited extract from his Australia Day address in 2016 based on the topic 'freedom from fear', and then answer the questions provided.

> Let me share with you parts of my story. It may be unfamiliar to those who have been born and grown up in a peaceful Australia. To those who have come as refugees from the world's trouble spots, parts of this story will be too familiar. A point of this story is to emphasise how very lucky we are to enjoy freedom from fear, and how very unlucky are many, many others who neither choose, nor deserve their fate.

I was born in a small fishing village called Malek, in the South Sudan … as a young boy, about the age of a typical second grader in Sydney, I was conscripted into an army.

As they took me away from my home and family I didn't even understand what freedoms I had lost. I didn't understand how fearful I should have been. I was young. I was ignorant. I lost the freedom to read and write. I lost the freedom to sing children's songs. I lost the right to be innocent. I lost the right to be a child …

To those recently arrived, do not give up the dream that brought you here. Within every Australian community there are people who were immigrants or whose parents were immigrants. Treat the experiences that brought you here as tough training for the journey of establishing new lives, new families, new careers …

1 What do you think is the main **purpose** of the speech? Provide reasons for your answer.

____

____

2 Who do you think is the target audience of the speech?

____

____

Visual persuasion

Visual language is an important part of many persuasive texts, especially websites and advertisements. When studying any visual text, think about the effects of the following elements.

- **Main colours**: do these colours make you think of any qualities or ideas? For example, the colour green might make you think of nature and the environment, while red might make you think of love or anger.
- **Symbolism**: what is used to represent ideas in the image? For example, a red rose might **symbolise** romance.
- **Framing**: what is included in the image? What has been left out?
- **Camera angles** or **shot types**: is the subject captured from above or far away, making it seem small and weak, or is a close-up being used to highlight a specific detail?

purpose An intended or assumed reason for a type of text
symbolism The use of one object, person or situation to signify or represent another, by giving them meanings that are different from their literal sense (e.g. a dove is a symbol of peace)

3.5

Check for understanding

Earth Hour is a campaign to raise awareness about global warming. It was launched in Sydney in 2007 and has since become a worldwide phenomenon, with over 190 countries participating. Here are three different Earth Hour poster advertisements.

The table below has been partially filled in for you using the first Earth Hour poster. Choose *one* of the other two posters and fill in the remaining column of the table in dot-point form.

Feature	Poster 1	Poster 2
main colours	› warm colours of red, orange and yellow on left, contrasting with cool green colours on right in background › black rectangle to frame main message with blue Earth standing out against the black outer space	
symbolism	› wi-fi symbol positioned over planet Earth, suggesting it is impacting on or dominating Earth › blazing fire and flaming trees on left contrast with the healthy, green forest trees on the right, suggesting the destructive consequences of electrical energy and climate change	
framing	› images of nature frame the central message and written text details on all sides, drawing attention to the important information and the central image of Earth dwarfed by a wi-fi symbol	

Feature	Poster 1	Poster 2
angle or shot type	› extreme long shot makes Earth looks small and vulnerable from outer space	

Identifying purpose and audience

The purpose of a persuasive text is its intended reason for existing – *why* it has been created. While the obvious purpose behind a persuasive text might be to persuade others to think or do something, a persuasive text also can aim to fulfil other purposes, such as:

- to raise awareness
- to change the actions or behaviours of others
- to educate others
- to frighten or warn others
- to get others to think

When thinking about persuasive texts, try to also identify the specific audience being targeted. The target audience is the groups or individuals that the text is trying to convince, for example, Australian teenagers, the elderly, the unemployed, parents of babies, or dog-lovers. In order to identify the target audience of a persuasive text, you may need to think about:

» the type of language or techniques used

» the values and attitudes being appealed to

» where the persuasive text might be read or listened to.

Audience values and attitudes

Certain audiences may have different **values** and **attitudes** from each other. Values are the principles and ideals that we most care about. Values influence our attitudes. For instance:

» Kate values education, and this is obvious in her dedicated attitude towards her studies.

» The high value that Rae placed on money led to his attitude that working overtime was worth it for the extra pay.

» The way they valued adventure meant they had a positive attitude towards travel.

Persuasive texts work by appealing to our values and attitudes. The Earth Hour posters appeal to the fact that the audience values the environment and therefore has the attitude that climate action is important.

values Ideas and beliefs specific to individuals and groups
attitudes Particular ways of thinking and feeling towards people or things

UNIT 4

Who are you? How would you define yourself? What groups do you identify with? This unit will help you explore the important concept of identity and examine how personal and social identities are expressed in texts. Understanding your own identity is key to exploring the representations of people, ideas and events in texts, and in recognising how or why you respond to them in certain ways. The activities in this unit will therefore also assist you to think about influences that shape the person you are.

In this unit you will learn:

- what identity is
- to recognise how personal and social identities are expressed in texts
- to understand what influences shape your own identity.

Curriculum content

Australian Curriculum content description	Content code
Understand how language expresses and creates personal and social identities.	AC9E7LA01
Explain the effect of current technology on reading, creating and responding to texts including media texts.	AC9E7LY01

What is identity?

Let's start with some simple definitions of the word 'identity'.

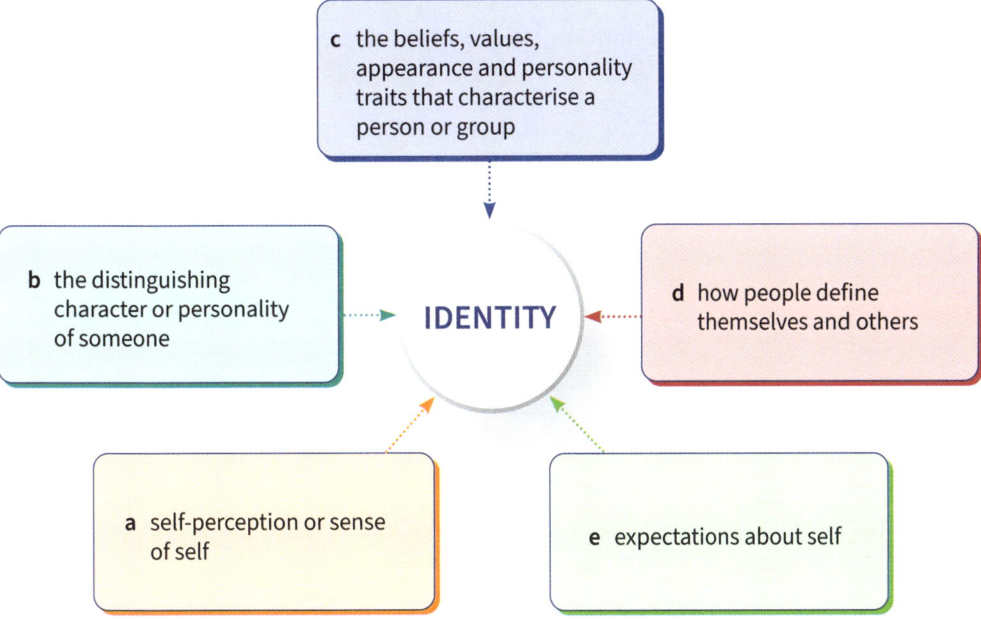

4.1 Reflecting and discussing

Discuss the following questions in pairs, in small groups or with the whole class, as directed by your teacher.

1 Which of the definitions do you find the most useful in understanding the concept of identity?

2 What is your understanding of identity? Explain in your own words.

3 What personality traits, interests and behaviours make up your identity?

Of course, the word 'identity' can be used in a range of different ways, and its meaning is dependent on these **contexts**. Read the following sentences that include the word *identity*.

» The **values** of mateship and 'a fair go' are part of our Australian national *identity*. ______

» A love of reading is part of my *identity*. ______

» Her caring nature was an important part of her *identity*. ______

» In a case of mistaken *identity*, the wrong person was arrested. ______

» His *identity* as a businessman was reflected by his suit, tie and briefcase. ______

context An environment or situation (social, cultural or historical) in which a text is responded to or created. Or wording surrounding an unfamiliar word, which a reader or listener uses to understand its meaning
values Ideas and beliefs specific to individuals and groups

4.2

Check for understanding

1 Think about how each of the sentences relates to the previous definitions of identity provided. Place the letter/s of each definition beside the sentences that they best match.

2 Write three sentences of your own that use the word 'identity'.

a ____

____

b ____

____

c ____

____

Personal and social identities

While each of us might have our own personal identity based on what makes us who we are as an individual, such as our appearance, interests, personality traits and so on, we are also likely to belong to a range of social groups. Social groups are those that we identify and interact with, usually because we share some situations with them. Some social groups include:

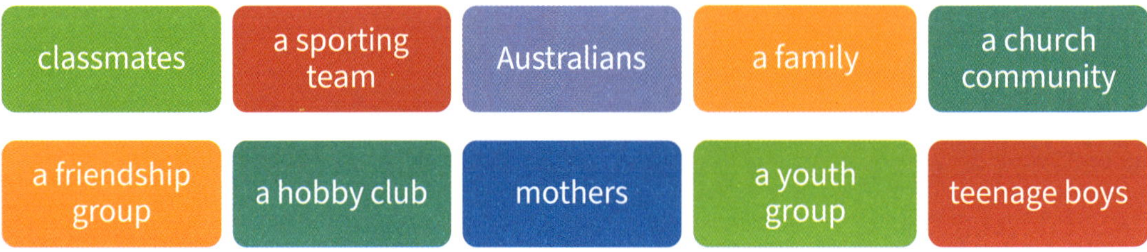

Look at the table below that illustrates the differences between personal and social identities.

Personal identity	Social identity
how you see yourself as an individual	how you see yourself belonging to a certain group
your difference from others	your similarity to others in a group
your sense of self	your sense of belonging
influences on personal identity: interests, hobbies, personality traits, experiences, etc.	influences on social identity: age, religion, race, ethnicity, social class, nationality, gender, etc.

Some influences on personal identity also contribute to your social identity and vice versa. That's because there is an overlap between personal and social identities. Part of your personal identity may be that you are a tween or a teenager – which makes you see yourself as *different* from adults or the elderly – but you may also feel a sense of belonging to the social group of tweens or teens because you are *similar* to them and may be experiencing the same milestones or challenges.

4.3 Get creative

In the space below, create an identity profile by identifying aspects of your personal and social identity *or* aspects of the personal and social identity of a character in a book you have read or a film you have watched.

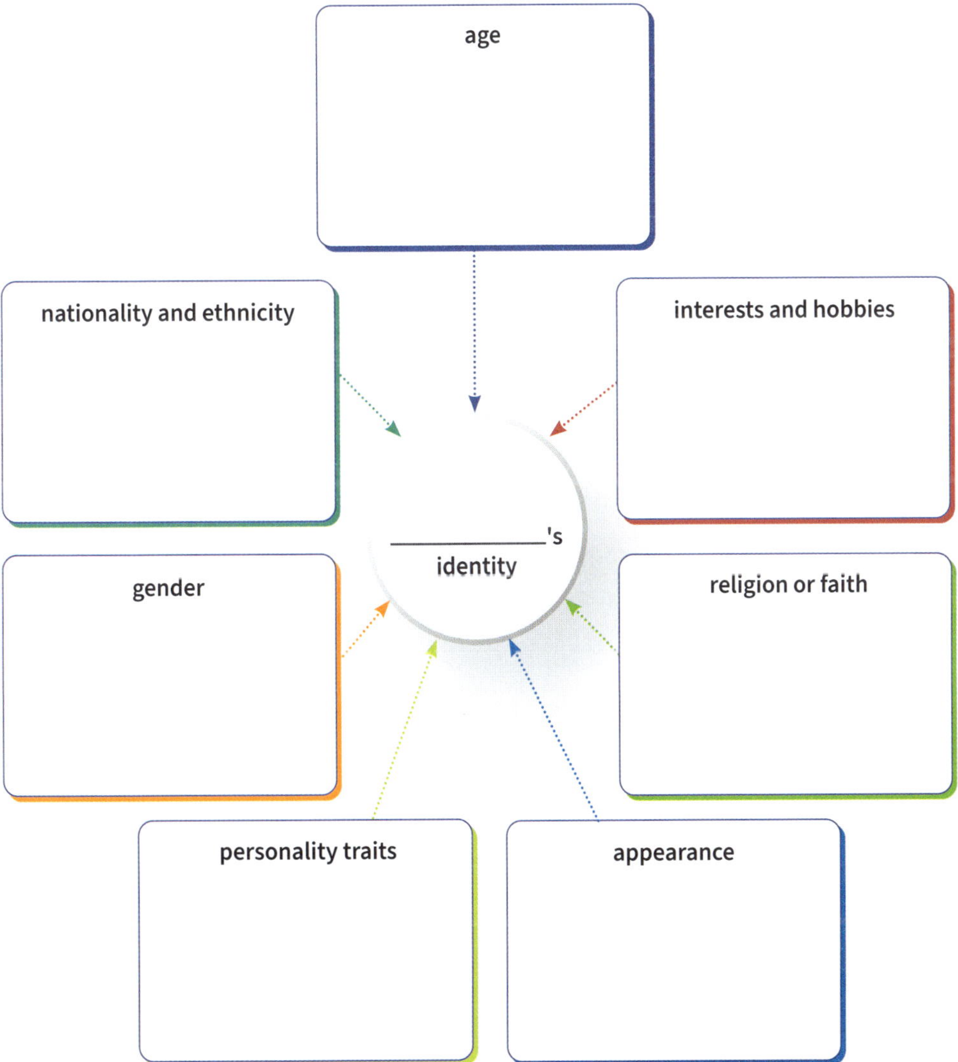

Understanding how identities are expressed

The personal and social identities of non-fiction authors/subjects and fictional characters in texts are expressed in lots of ways, including through:

- names
- language
- appearance and clothing
- actions.

Identity and names

Our names contribute a great deal to our identity. One example of the relationship between a name and identity is that of Oodgeroo Noonuccal, one of Australia's most influential First Nations writers and artists. She devoted her life to telling the stories of First Nations Australians – in writing, in visual art, through a rich oral tradition and through her involvement in Aboriginal civil rights. Oodgeroo Noonuccal was born Kathleen Jean Mary Ruska in 1920. After she married and started publishing her writing, she was known as Kath Walker. In 1988, she changed her name to Oodgeroo ('paperbark tree') Noonuccal (after her ancestors and home), in recognition of her Aboriginal heritage.

4.4 Reflecting and discussing

Discuss the following questions in pairs, in small groups or with the whole class, as directed by your teacher.

1 Why do you think Oodgeroo Noonuccal felt her new name was a better expression of her identity than 'Kath Walker'?

2 Do you think your name suits you and your identity? Give reasons for your answer.

The names of fictional characters in stories can also tell us a lot about their identities. Some authors use a charactonym. This means that the name of the character reveals something about them or their personality. Look at the following examples from famous novels or films.

- Luke Skywalker: the **protagonist** of *Star Wars*, a film set in space and created by George Lucas.
- Ebenezer Scrooge: the main character in the novella *A Christmas Carol* by Charles Dickens. A scrooge is a mean, miserly person who hates spending money.
- Sir Toby Belch: a cheerful character in Shakespeare's *Twelfth Night* who consumes excessive amounts of food, wine and ale (beer).

protagonist The main character in a text

Storytelling

Humans have shared stories for thousands of years. Every time you tell a friend what you did on the weekend, you become a storyteller too. Ancient stories, called myths or legends, were passed down through generations in a range of ways: told around a fire, represented in picture form on cave walls, or performed using song, dance or puppets. Today, these stories continue to be told through new media. This unit will help you to be able to recognise and discuss the aesthetic and social value of literary texts. You will explore how language is used in stories to shape meaning and the way that it can vary according to audience and purpose.

In this unit you will learn:

- about the origins of storytelling
- how First Nations Australians' stories are told in a modern context
- what is meant by the 'aesthetic and social value' of stories, as well as how to recognise it.

Curriculum content

Australian Curriculum content description	Content code
Identify and explore ideas, points of view, characters, events and/or issues in literary texts, drawn from historical, social and/or cultural contexts, by First Nations Australian, and wide-ranging Australian and world authors.	AC9E7LE01
Discuss the aesthetic and social value of literary texts using relevant and appropriate metalanguage.	AC9E7LE04
Explain the effect of current technology on reading, creating and responding to texts including media texts.	AC9E7LY01
Analyse the ways in which language features shape meaning and vary according to audience and purpose.	AC9E7LY03

context An environment or situation (social, cultural or historical) in which a text is responded to or created. Or wording surrounding an unfamiliar word, which a reader or listener uses to understand its meaning

Storytelling histories

Storytelling was originally an oral tradition, which means stories were shared in spoken words between humans. Pictures and performances of stories also have a long history in human civilisation. It is believed that writing began in Mesopotamia around 3400 BCE using cuneiform (marks on wet clay), followed by Egyptian hieroglyphs soon after. This invention of a new way to tell stories would change our world forever.

Most of the world's earliest stories were in the following forms:

5.1 Check for understanding

1 Research the difference between a myth and a legend and explain your findings below.

____

____

____

2 Provide definitions for the following types of stories.

a fable

____

____

b fairytale

____

____

c parable

____

____

d epics and sagas

____

____

e folktale

3 The following stories continue to be told many years after their first telling. Complete the table below. You may need to conduct some research to find out more about the stories.

Story title	Origin	Summary of story
'Pandora's Box'	Greek mythology	
'The Rainbow Serpent'		
'Gilgamesh'		
'Robin Hood'		
'Momotarō'		
'Noah's Ark'		

5.2 Get creative

1 Select one story from the table above and retell a scene from it in multimodal form for an **audience** of your peers. You could use a combination of hand-drawn images and written words or digital tools to create your chosen scene.

2 Swap your story scene with someone else and complete the following checklist based on their story.

Elements of multimodal story	Tick if included
a title	
at least two modes (e.g. writing, speaking, visual images)	
language suited to the target audience of peers	
a plot event, a setting and characters	

audience An intended or assumed group of readers, listeners or viewers that a writer, designer, filmmaker or speaker is addressing

Creation stories

The Dreaming did not take place at the beginning of time – this is a common misconception. It encompasses the past, present and future; it is non-linear. As a holistic philosophy grounded in the very earth itself, it cannot be assigned to a past people. It is an integrated way of life that many First Nations peoples believe in and live by today.

The Dreaming is a unique world view that belongs to different First Nations peoples. A world view is a structured way of understanding reality through a collection of shared **values**, **attitudes** and rules. The Dreaming includes creation stories and beliefs about how things came into being. These stories have been passed on from one generation to the next for thousands of years in oral form or through song, dance and art. These creation stories and other Dreaming stories give us an important understanding of the world. Some Dreaming stories include:

values Ideas and beliefs specific to individuals and groups
attitudes Particular ways of thinking and feeling toward people or things

- 'The Rainbow Serpent'
- 'Whirlpool Song'
- 'Morning Star'
- 'The Wagalak Sisters'
- 'Namorrodor'.

5.3 Reflecting and discussing

Discuss the following questions in pairs, in small groups or with the whole class, as directed by your teacher.

1 Which of the Dreaming stories above do you know?

2 Read or watch animated versions of these stories online . What is your understanding of these stories? Share your experience with each other. The ABC's *Dust Echoes* series includes a great selection of Dreaming stories. Source them online.

3 What lessons about life and creation do you learn through the stories?

The impact of current technology on storytelling

In response to technological developments and new media, the way that stories are told has changed over the years. Digital technologies now allow us to engage with stories that include visual, written and auditory/aural **modes** all at the same time, like those in the *Dust Echoes* series above.

mode Various processes of communication – listening, speaking, reading or viewing and writing or creating

A beautiful **multimodal** version of the Dreaming story of Butu Wugun (Black Crow) and Wilbung (Magpie), voiced by Paul Teerman and animated by GuavaJagular, was produced as part of the 2020 NAIDOC Week program provided by the Casula Powerhouse Arts Centre in New South Wales. The language spoken is a mixture of **Standard Australian English** and Darug, a First Nations **dialect** that originated in New South Wales.

A selection of still images from the animated film are reproduced below. Carefully look at how their visual and written language work together to create meaning.

multimodal A combination of 2 or more communication modes (e.g. print, image and spoken text, as in film or computer presentations)
Standard Australian English Recognised as the 'common language' of Australians, it is the dynamic and evolving spoken and written English used for official or public purposes, and recorded in dictionaries, style guides and grammars
dialect Form of a language distinguished by features of vocabulary, grammar and pronunciation particular to a region

5.4 Check for understanding

1 How does the illustration reveal that the two birds are friends and brothers?

____

____

____

____

____

____

____

____

____

2 What visual techniques are used to show the battle between the birds in this image?

___

___

___

3 What is the impact of using both Darug language and English words to tell the story?

___

___

___

4 At the end of the story, Paul Teerman explains that every Dreaming story is told because it shares an important lesson. He says that the lesson in the story about Butu Wugun and Wilbung is that 'you should always do and be the best you can' and that you 'should respect the differences of those around you'. Do you agree that this is an important lesson to learn? Provide reasons.

___

___

The aesthetic value of literary texts

The word '**aesthetic**' means a sense of the artistic quality of a text. Recognising the 'aesthetic value' of a **literary text** is about appreciating its pleasurable, unusual, creative, moving or powerful aspects. Some scenes in a film may be visually mesmerising and interesting to watch, or the descriptions written in a poem or story might be especially lovely and evocative. Here are some sentences referring to the aesthetic value of texts.

aesthetic Concerned with a sense of beauty or an appreciation of artistic expression
literary text Past and contemporary texts across a range of cultural contexts which are valued for their form and style and are recognised as having artistic value
imagery Visually descriptive or figurative language to represent things including objects, actions and ideas in ways that appeal to the senses of the reader or viewer

- The aesthetic value of the poem lies in its engaging sensory **imagery** and rhyme.
- An aesthetically pleasing painting may be full of vibrant colour.
- The story is valued for its aesthetic qualities, such as clever use of figurative devices.

Discussing the aesthetic value of a text will require you to use appropriate language that shows your understanding of the importance and effects of certain techniques. In the sentences above, language like 'sensory imagery', 'rhyme', 'vibrant colour' and 'figurative devices' show an understanding of how a text is constructed to produce aesthetic effects. We call this type of technical vocabulary used to describe and analyse the language in a text '**metalanguage**'.

metalanguage Vocabulary including technical terms, concepts, ideas or codes used to describe or discuss a language. The language of grammar and the language of literary criticism are examples

5.5 Check for understanding

Match the following metalanguage terms with their possible aesthetic effects.

Metalanguage	Possible aesthetic effect
rhyme	produces a less saturated style of colour; might create a peaceful, calm or romantic atmosphere; might be associated with the femininity of a character
sensory imagery	creates an engaging, predictable and repetitive rhythm that is satisfying and pleasing to the ear; helps create a musical quality
pastel colour	engages the senses to develop a realistic, immersive setting or a vivid mental picture

5.6 Reflecting and discussing

Discuss the following questions in pairs, in small groups or with the whole class, as directed by your teacher.

1 What do you think makes children's nursery rhymes aesthetically pleasing to listen to?

2 What is a text you have enjoyed because it was beautiful, striking or constructed in an unusual way?

The social value of literary texts

Stories are valuable to our understanding of the world and our place in it. They teach us important lessons, take us into the lives of others and allow us to respond to real events. Therefore, stories have social value. Here are some examples of sentences about the 'social value' of texts.

- The social value of the novel *Wonder* can be attributed to the important lessons it teaches us about accepting others.
- The novel *Goodnight Mister Tom* holds social value because it allows us a glimpse into life during World War II.
- *The Little Refugee* provides a valuable insight into the experiences of refugees in society.

Some texts become very important to a society because they capture a certain moment in time or a world view that helps us better understand human nature. This is why Shakespeare's plays continue to have such significant social value. Novels like *To Kill a Mockingbird* by Harper Lee, *Lord of the Flies* by William Golding and *The Adventures of Huckleberry Finn* by Mark Twain are still studied and enjoyed today, albeit from a more critical point of view that sometimes seeks to interrogate the now dated or offensive representations or use of language.

Telling your story

We all have stories to tell. Some people's stories are happy and heartwarming; others' stories are inspiring or even difficult. Chloé Hayden is an actor, social media star and disability advocate. In order to help other neurodivergent young people, Chloé decided to share her own story of growing up with autism and ADHD. Her book, *Different, Not Less: A neurodivergent's guide to embracing your true self and finding your happily ever after*, combines autobiography and helpful advice.

In this unit you will learn:

- the difference between autobiography and biography
- what is meant by a 'hybrid text'
- about Latin and Greek word origins
- how to maintain verb tense.

Curriculum content

Australian Curriculum content description	Content code
Understand how language expresses and creates personal and social identities.	AC9E7LA01
Understand how consistency of tense through verbs and verb groups achieves clarity in sentences.	AC9E7LA06
Create and edit literary texts that experiment with language features and literary devices encountered in texts.	AC9E7LE07
Plan, create, rehearse and deliver presentations for purposes and audiences in ways that may be imaginative, reflective, informative, persuasive and/or analytical, by selecting text structures, language features, literary devices and visual features, and using features of voice including volume, tone, pitch and pace.	AC9E7LY07

Extract from *Different, Not Less*

Read the following extract from Chloé Hayden's book.

My parents called me 'our quirky little genius', 'our princess and the pea child'. This was because every night I was lost in my encyclopedias, later rambling about the facts I'd learned to anyone who cared (or didn't care) to listen. I would cry at the smallest sign of a tag touching my skin. And I couldn't make a single friend unless it was a snail I'd picked up on a path and begged to keep as a best friend.

I didn't fit in at school, my teachers often calling my parents to let them know that I'd spent all day hiding in the back of the library or in the toilet. I couldn't wear certain clothes, or deal with certain textures–my outfit of choice was Kmart tracksuits with the tags cut off. The only food that passed my lips was white, bland and less than two ingredients. (Pasta with cheese? Fine. White bread and butter? Great. Don't even *think* about adding something else into the mix, though.)

I didn't have any friends, nor did I care to try making them, and would instead be spellbound for hours in my books or make-believe worlds, which no one else was authorised to enter. I'd speak out of turn, lecturing adults as a seven-year-old and letting them know that their hair was messy, or that something they'd said was untrue, or that they were unkind. Other times, I'd go out of my way to tell every stranger I saw how pretty they were. And sometimes I wasn't able to speak at all, becoming mute.

Routine and structure were important; perish the thought of plans or routines changing. Something as small as dinner being ten minutes later than when Mum had said it would be, or the time of my weekly horse-riding lessons being moved would cause a panic equivalent to being caught in the headlights of an oncoming car...

Despite all of this, to my parents and those who surrounded me, I was just *Chloé*. A bit sensitive, a bit quirky, a bit off the cuff. And, after all, what child isn't a bit of an oddball?

To me, though? It felt like I had crash-landed on an alien planet, a world that seemed similar enough to my own that I was able to fake it for a few years, but distant enough that I felt like a complete and utter freak. It was as though everyone else had figured out the rules of this planet, but the rocket scientists back home had forgotten to give me the handbook, and it was entirely up to me to figure them out.

People on this planet were horribly, ridiculously confusing, and everything seemed like it was out to destroy my entire being. The lights were atrociously loud and blindingly bright. The people said things they didn't mean at all ('It's raining cats and dogs' apparently did not mean a hailstorm of puppies and kittens, much to my twelve-year-old self's disappointment). There were social 'rules' that everyone had to follow, even though they didn't make any sense and, if you broke them, people treated you as if you had just broken some secret, ancient code.

Eye contact? Small talk? And why are you people so touch oriented?

None of it made any sense. Even still, none of it makes sense.

6.1 Check for understanding

1 From looking at the extract, how do you know it is an autobiography rather than a biography? Tick the most appropriate answer.

a The story is about Chloé Hayden's life. ☐

b The writer uses first-person narration (I, me, we). ☐

c The writer did a lot of research into Chloé Hayden's life. ☐

d The writer interviewed Chloé Hayden. ☐

2 List three words that start with the prefix 'bio'.

____

3 List three words that start with the prefix 'auto'.

____

4 Based on the words above, can you come up with a hypothesis (suggestion) about what these prefixes mean?

a bio ______________________________

b auto ______________________________

5 What is the dictionary definition for each of the following terms?

a autobiography ______________________________

b biography ______________________________

6 What do you think the following words mean? Use a dictionary, or predict the meanings based on how the writer uses them in the extract above.

a rambling ______________________________

b bland ______________________________

c perish ______________________________

d quirky ______________________________

7 What difficulties did Chloé face in her childhood? List three challenges she experienced.

____

____

____

8 What does Chloé mean when she says that to her parents, she was just Chloé?

____

____

Latin and Greek word origins

Many words in English come to us from the classical languages of Greek and Latin. Often these are scientific or technical terms, because scientists and philosophers continued to use these languages long after everyday people stopped speaking them. However, you might be surprised to know that some very common words also come to us from these ancient languages, such as butter, which comes from Greek words meaning 'cow cheese'!

bous (cow) + *turos* (cheese) = butter

In the 'Author's note' in *Different, Not Less,* Chloé Hayden explains that neurodiversity describes 'the natural variation of brain function and behavioural differences that exist among humans, including conditions such as autism, ADHD, dyslexia and dyspraxia.'

The term 'neurodiverse' comes from one Greek word and one Latin word:

neuro
from a Greek word
meaning 'of the nervous system' or 'brain'

\+

diversus
from a Latin word
meaning 'various' or 'different'

Similarly, 'dyslexia' and 'dyspraxia' come from Greek roots:

dys
from a Greek word
meaning 'impaired function' or 'difficulty'

\+

lexis
from a Greek word
meaning 'words' or 'speech'

\+

praxis
from a Greek word
meaning 'to act'

Studying word origins is known as 'etymology', which comes from two Greek words: *etymos* (true or actual) and *logia* (a study of). This became *etymologia*, which was borrowed by Latin to mean the study of a word's true origin.

6.2 Check for understanding

Look up these root words in a dictionary to find their origins. You could also search an online etymology dictionary. An example has been done for you.

Root	Origin	Meaning	Examples
hal	Latin	breath	inhale, exhale, halitosis
acro			
aqua			

Root	Origin	Meaning	Examples
cardio			
cycl			
luna			

Hybrid texts

Rather than being a straightforward autobiography, *Different, Not Less* is a **hybrid text**, combining the story of Chloé's life with advice for other neurodiverse young people. 'Hybrid' comes from a Latin word meaning the offspring of two different species. A hybrid text combines or blends two different types of text; in this case, an autobiography and an informational text.

hybrid text A composite text resulting from a purposeful mixing of elements from different sources or genres (e.g. 'infotainment')

6.3 Check for understanding

1 Use the internet to find out what types of texts are combined in these hybrid texts.

Hybrid text	... is a combination of ...	
docudrama		
infomercial		
podcast		
'Booktok'		

2 Can you think of any other types of texts that might be considered hybrid texts?

____

____

Understanding verb tense

When writing about your own or someone else's life, it is likely that you will consider events that are in the past as well as the present, and maybe even hopes for the future. It is important, however, that writers maintain consistent use of tense in their writing.

Simple tenses

Verb tenses are a way of telling when an action happened or will happen. There are three simple tenses: past, present and future.

Past	Present	Future
Milo **ate** lasagne for dinner.	Milo **eats** lasagne for dinner.	Milo **will eat** lasagne for dinner.

6.4

Check for understanding

1 Identify the tense used in these sentences by circling the correct answer.

Carrie walked her dog before school.	past/present/future
The Kangaroos will win the grand final.	past/present/future
My family went to Kakadu over the holidays.	past/present/future
Moh studies hard for her tests.	past/present/future

2 Change the following sentences to past tense.

a Ali enjoys swimming at the beach.

____

b The movie is really exciting.

____

c We accidentally kick the soccer ball over the fence.

____

d Elena receives a medal for taekwondo.

____

More complex tenses

We can also use different verb groups that include special words called 'auxiliary' or 'helping' verbs along with the main verb. Auxiliary verbs are various forms of the words 'be' or 'have'.

For example, when we say 'I **am** playing' or 'He **is** eating', we are using the present continuous tense, which tells us that the action is happening now. When we say 'I **had** eaten' or 'They **had** finished', we are using the past perfect tense, which tells us that the action happened before another action in the past.

By using different verb groups, we can tell people exactly when something happened or is happening, which helps us to communicate our ideas better.

	Past	Present	Future
Simple	I **cleaned** my room yesterday.	I **clean** my room every day.	I **will clean** my room tomorrow.
Perfect	I **had cleaned** my room before I played on my phone.	I **have cleaned** my room a lot this week.	I **will have cleaned** my room at least 20 times this month.
Continuous	I **was cleaning** my room when I got distracted by my phone.	I **am cleaning** my room while playing games on my phone.	I **will be cleaning** my room forever at this rate.
Perfect continuous	I **had been cleaning** my room since I was a child.	I **have been cleaning** my room since I woke up this morning.	I **will have been cleaning** my room for days by the time I finish.

6.5 Check for understanding

1 Highlight the verb groups in the following sentences:

a She is cooking dinner for her family.

b They were playing soccer in the park.

c He has been studying for his exams all week.

d We will have finished the project by next Friday.

e I had never seen such a beautiful sunset before.

2 Write down the verb tense of the following sentences:

a Aunt Sarah will sing a song. ______________________________

b I am reading an awesome book. ______________________________

c They have played a great football game. ______________________________

d Thomas had eaten breakfast. ______________________________

e We will be going to the beach. ______________________________

3 Choose the correct verb tense for the following sentences:

a I (am/was) ______________________________ feeling sick yesterday.

b They (will/would) ____________________ visit their grandparents next weekend.

c Eden (has/had) ____________________ already finished her homework tonight.

d We (are/were) ______________________________ going to New Zealand tomorrow.

e Riley (has/had) ____________________ been practising piano for two hours when we arrived.

Modal verbs

modal verb A verb that expresses a degree of probability attached by a speaker or writer to a statement (e.g. 'I might come home') or a degree of obligation (e.g. 'You must give it to me')

Modal verbs are another type of auxiliary verb that combine with regular verbs. Modal verbs modify the meaning of the original verb by expressing ability, permission, obligation, possibility and advice.

The most common modal verbs are 'can', 'could', 'may', 'might', 'must', 'should', 'shall', 'will' and 'would'.

For example:

» I **can speak** Indonesian.

» It **might rain** later today.

» Daisy **should eat** more green vegetables.

» You **will take** the rubbish out.

6.6

Check for understanding

1 Complete the sentences with the appropriate modal verb:

a You (should/might) ________________ study harder if you want to do well.

b He (must/should) ________________ have finished his homework by now.

c I (can/could) ________________ speak Italian fluently.

d (Could/May) ________________ I use your computer, please?

e We (might/can) ________________ go to the beach tomorrow if the weather is nice.

2 In your notebook, write a short paragraph about what you can and can't do. Use at least three different modal verbs in your paragraph.

» Example: I can speak English and Chinese fluently, but I can't play the guitar very well. I should practise more if I want to improve. I also can't eat spicy food because it makes my mouth burn.

Writing your story

In the passage below, Chloé Hayden explains that writing about your own life should have three stages, just like a fairytale:

1 The **Once Upon a Time stage**, an introduction, an opening to a new adventure, the promise of something new. Fairytales need beginnings that aren't all sunflowers and butterflies — imagine if every fairytale started off with a happy protagonist backed by a joyful soundtrack and no evil lion uncles, sorcerers or poisoned apples in sight. Would that even be a story at all? Despite how much it

may hurt, our Once Upon a Time needs to start somewhere challenging, maybe even a bit bleak, to launch us into our second stage.

2 The **Adventure stage** is about confronting dragons, great journeys and courageous battles. Your Adventure might not be with a fire-breathing beast, but perhaps it's with poor circumstances, ill mental health, a lack of accessibility and understanding, or a world of other challenges. Our Adventure is where our stories begin to come together: we meet our sidekicks, we find the path to figure out who we are, and we begin to discover where our place is in the world.

3 And finally, if Disney has taught me anything, it's that if you think your fairytale is finished but you haven't reached your **Happily Ever After stage** yet, you are still only in the beginning chapters and you have many stages to go. A book cannot close without a Happily Ever After; a fairytale movie cannot end without a triumphant orchestral finale. And regardless of whatever happened during your Once Upon a Time or your Adventure stages, the same holds true for you: your Happily Ever After will come.

And the best part? Unlike traditional fairytales, in which every final page is exactly the same, *your* fairytale is not a closed book.

6.7 Reflecting and discussing

Discuss the following questions in pairs, in small groups or with the whole class, as directed by your teacher.

1 What do you think of Chloé's suggested structure for writing your story? Can you see how the story of a person's life can be structured in this way?

2 What events have happened in your life that might be considered 'Adventures'? Are there any challenges or conflicts that you have experienced?

6.8 Get creative

1 'This is my story': in your notebook, write an autobiographical scene from your life in 300–500 words. Rehearse and then deliver a brief oral presentation from that scene or as a follow up to it.

» First, think of a moment that is strong in your memory. It might be a funny, sad, scary, painful, proud or happy memory.

» How will you present? Video or podcast? What will work best for your audience?

» When was this? Where were you? Who were you with? What happened? What was the weather like? How did you feel?

UNIT 7

Appreciating poetry

Poetry is an important part of our culture. It is a concise and imaginative form of writing through which poets explore ideas, issues and viewpoints that are important to them. By using a range of poetic devices, poets can pack a lot of meaning into just a few words.

In this unit you will learn:

- about poetic devices
- how meaning is created in poetry
- how to write a poem analysis.

Curriculum content

Australian Curriculum content description	Content code
Investigate the role of vocabulary in building specialist and technical knowledge, including terms that have both everyday and technical meanings.	AC9E7LA08
Identify and explore ideas, points of view, characters, events and/or issues in literary texts, drawn from historical, social and/or cultural contexts, by First Nations Australian, and wide-ranging Australian and world authors.	AC9E7LE01
Identify and explain how literary devices create layers of meaning in texts including poetry.	AC9E7LE06

Creating an image

Poetry is often at its most effective when it creates strong **imagery**. Imagery refers to the use of language to create vivid pictures in the reader's mind. Read this poem by Grace Perry and try to picture the situation she is depicting.

imagery Visually descriptive or figurative language to represent things including objects, actions and ideas in ways that appeal to the senses of the reader or viewer

Face of the City

They are changing the face of the city;
old buildings of sandstone are tumbling down.
The drill bites deep till raw nerves tremble,
and steel on steel scream shatters ground.
Unanaesthetised but uncomplaining,
cavernous mouth and haunted eyes
feel each shiver of wide incisions,
retracted muscles quivering
as rough hands chisel at splintered bone,
and a whistle shrills for the man suspended
above the ruined and broken stones.

7.1 Reflecting and discussing

Discuss the following questions in pairs, in small groups or with the whole class, as directed by your teacher.

1 What makes poetry different from other forms of writing? How would you define poetry?

2 Identify three songs that you enjoy listening to. What do you like about these songs? Are there any qualities that they have in common with poetry?

7.2 Check for understanding

1 Use a dictionary to find the definitions of the following words from 'Face of the City':

a unanaesthetised ____________________

b cavernous ____________________

c incisions ____________________

d retracted ____________________

2 What situation or issue do you think Grace Perry is depicting? Write a single sentence to explain the central idea in this poem.

____

____

3 Perry uses a number of strong verbs to depict actions in this poem, such as ‘tumbling’, ‘bites’ and ‘tremble’. Identify three more strong verbs used in the poem.

____

4 Through her careful and deliberate choice of words, Perry creates a striking atmosphere in this city scene. Which words best describe this atmosphere?

- a calm and peaceful ☐
- b violent and harsh ☐
- c energetic and busy ☐
- d moody and bleak ☐

5 **Alliteration** refers to the repetition of consonant sounds, usually at the beginnings of words.

a ‘The drill bites deep till raw nerves tremble’ repeats ‘d’ and ‘t’ sounds. How does this help suggest the sound of a pneumatic drill?

____

____

b ‘and steel on steel scream shatters ground’ repeats the ‘s’ sound. How does this help suggest the sound of metal scraping on metal?

____

____

6 **Assonance** refers to the repetition of vowel sounds within words. Use a green highlighter to identify where Perry repeats the ‘i’ sound several times in just four lines.

7 The poem uses imagery of a literal face to represent the appearance of the city. Highlight the words in the poem that refer to parts of a human face.

8 ‘Unanaesthetised’ is a technical word you may not expect to find in a poem. Why do you think Perry chooses to use it here?

____

____

9 Why do you think Perry uses the image of a human face being destroyed to comment on the changes being made to the city? Do you think this makes readers react more strongly?

___

___

___

___

alliteration A recurrence of the same consonant sounds at the beginning of words in close succession (e.g. 'ripe, red raspberry')
assonance The repetition of vowel sounds within words (e.g. rain, main)

Making a point

Poetry can be a powerful way to engage with important social issues because it allows us to express complex ideas and emotions in a creative and impactful way. Poets use language, imagery and sound to communicate their thoughts and feelings, and often use their work to shed light on issues such as discrimination, inequality and injustice. By reading and writing poetry about these issues, we can develop a deeper understanding of the world around us and explore our own feelings and perspectives. Poetry can inspire us to take action and make positive changes in our communities, making it an important tool for creating social awareness and promoting social justice.

In the Forest

Wait for the axe sound in the forest.
The birds wait. The lizards pause
and wait. The creatures that are nearest
earth feel the approaching pace

measure a man. And they must wait.
Then has the time come? The dark
of forest is so solid that
its inter-growth should never break.

But has the time come? The birds
are nervous, see them flinch and turn.
The snake moves into the reeds
quickly. Danger, the signs warn.

That! Slap of an axe. Slap!
There, quick, over there. The tree

is tensed. In its green height
the possums clutch their young; they flee.

Crack again crack of slow man's weapon,
intolerable wait for the one tree's sake
for its grasping fall and its death to happen
and the gash in the forest, and light to break.

Now, says the axe, and the tree is fallen,
the spider crushed in its secret nest.
The late slow lives have been taken,
in the sheltering tree they have been crushed.

The accepted world is quickly broken,
the skull of the forest is opened up.
Now, means the axe. But the birds have forgotten –
there are other trees; they prepare for sleep.

7.3 Check for understanding

1 Look up the following words from 'In the Forest' in the dictionary and write down their definitions:

a flinch ______________________________

b intolerable ______________________________

2 What was your emotional reaction to this poem? Circle the word that best describes your response.

anger	apathy	pity
nostalgia	regret	sadness

3 The poem is literally about a tree being cut down in a forest. Its theme, however, is about a broader issue.

a Identify three outcomes that result from the tree being felled.

____

____

____

b Which creatures escape the felling of the tree? Which don't?

____

____

____

Poetic forms and devices

Poetic forms

Poetry comes in many forms, each with their own structures and styles. A form might have a set number of lines, a particular rhyme scheme (pattern) or subject matter that a poet typically uses when creating that type of poem. Some poets, however, choose not to use a specific form, instead writing in an unstructured way or creating a structure unique to them. This is called 'free verse'.

7.4 Get creative

A haiku is a simple, unrhymed Japanese poem. It has just three short lines and a total of 17 syllables – five in the first line, seven in the second line and five in the third line (5–7–5). Its cleverness lies in its ability to convey a lot of meaning and create vivid images in our minds using very few words. Traditionally, haikus were inspired by objects, events and phenomena in the natural world.

Both plains and mountains Have been captured by the snow There is nothing left – Jōsō	An evening cloudburst sparrows cling desperately to trembling bushes – Buson

1 Divide the haikus above into syllables to check that they conform to the 5–7–5 structure. A syllable is a single unit of sound in a word. For example, the word 'syllable' itself has three beats or syllables: syll/a/ble.

2 Write your own haiku about your favourite type of weather or season using the instructions below.

a Write a short descriptive paragraph in prose (not poetry) describing your chosen subject.

____

____

____

____

b Circle the most interesting or emotive words in your paragraph.

c Underline the least interesting descriptive words in your paragraph, and then look them up in a thesaurus to find a better alternative. Write each alternative above the original in your paragraph.

d Edit your paragraph down into three lines that use the most interesting descriptions. Write your three lines below.

____

e Count the syllables and alter your poem to make it fit the 5–7–5 structure. Write your completed haiku below.

7.5 Check for understanding

Research the following poetic forms and write down their main characteristics.

limerick	
sonnet	
ballad	
ode	
concrete poetry	

Poetic devices

Poetic devices are the language techniques that poets use to add impact and meaning to their writing. With so few words in most poems, poetic devices can be a way to really pack a punch!

7.6 Check for understanding

1 Write the poetic devices from the following list next to their correct definitions.

rhyme	rhythm	alliteration	assonance
onomatopoeia	simile	metaphor	symbol
personification	enjambment		

a a comparison in which one thing is described as being similar to something else, using the words 'like or 'as' ______ b a pattern of stressed or emphasised beats in a line of poetry ________________

____

c giving living qualities to a non-living thing ______________________________

d repeating the initial consonant sounds at the beginning of words that are in close proximity ____

e words that mimic the sounds they describe ___________________________

f an object or image that represents something else, often an abstract concept ____

g the repetition of vowel sounds in words that are in close proximity __________

____

h a pattern where words have the same or similar end sounds ________________

____

i a comparison where one thing is depicted as being something else _________

____

j the continuation of a phrase or sentence beyond the end of a line break

____

2 Complete the following table by finding examples of these poetic devices from 'Face of the City' and 'In the Forest'. Try to find more than one example of each.

	'Face of the City'	'In the Forest'
Personification		
Symbol		
Enjambment		
Alliteration		

3 Using a simile, metaphor or symbol, write two lines of poetry about a pet or your favourite possession.

____

____

4 Using alliteration, assonance or rhyme, write two lines of poetry about your favourite activity or hobby.

____

____

Verse novels

Some authors choose to write their novels using language features and structures usually associated with poetry. These are called 'verse novels', which differentiates them from novels written in the more traditional style known as 'prose'.

Run, by Australian author and poet Tim Sinclair, is a thriller verse novel set in Sydney. Dee is a teenager who loves parkour, which combines running and acrobatic feats to move quickly through the environment. Dee, however, gets caught up in a mystery, and he is soon running for his life. *Run* is written in the poetic form known as 'concrete poetry'.

This extract presents the reader with Dee running through the city and almost getting hit by a car.

I DROP
AND LAND on greasy steel, immediate roll
with no margin for error, back on my feet and run.
ALIVE WITH IT NOW, EXULTANT. The streets far
below me. My feet where nobody's should be.

It's mine alone, this space, this time. But up ahead,
danger. A schedule change, a dazzling light ...

And now I run for my life. Cliché slams my feet into
unforgiving metal, brake screams tear my eardrums.

One more step

barely enough –
a desperate jump,
a sideways lurch,
halfslip headlong
into a straggle of tree.
Branches
whipping my face,
bark cutting
my palms,
swaying and barely
supporting my weight,

but holding.
Breaking
the terror
of gravity.
I slither
down,
hardly noticing
the cuts and grazes,
thinking
only of escape.
Of solid ground
of feet hitting dirt
and running to concrete,
full feet sprinting to get out of here,
away from fear, from failure …

I run.
Away.
Moving dark, fast, slippery,
desperate to be
an ordinary part
of the night.

7.7 Reflecting and discussing

Discuss the following questions in pairs, in small groups or with the whole class, as directed by your teacher.

1 Based on this extract, how would you describe parkour? Is it something that seems exciting? Dangerous? Both?

2 How does Tim Sinclair manipulate the line structure of his poetry to create a sense of energy and speed in this extract?

3 Do you think you would enjoy reading a novel written in verse like this, or do you prefer prose? What makes you feel this way?

Writing an analytical paragraph

When studying poetry, a good way to write a clear analytical paragraph is to use the TEEL formula:

» Topic sentence: write a concise sentence that outlines the meaning or effect created by the poetic device/s.

- Example: introduce a clear example from the poem.
- Explanation: explain how the poetic device works.
- Link: sum up the meaning or effect created, or link back to the poem's overall meaning.

The topic sentence identifies a poetic device and its effect.

The explanation shows how the poetic device creates the effect.

The extract from *Run* uses alliteration to create a sense of Dee's fear and panic. The poet repeats the 'f' sound in 'full feet sprinting to get out of here,/ away from fear, from failure'. This repeated sound links the action of Dee sprinting with his feelings of fear and failure. It also connects the two lines together, creating a fast pace that reflects Dee running away. The alliteration suggests the rush of panic Dee feels after nearly getting hit by a car.

The second sentence introduces an example of the poetic device.

The link sentence summarises the point of the paragraph.

7.8 Check for understanding

1 Use a dictionary to the find the following words and write their definitions here.

a exultant ______________________________

b cliché ______________________________

2 Which lines from the poem suggest that Dee is nearly hit by a car while doing parkour?

____

____

3 Why do you think Tim Sinclair changes from longer lines to very short ones after Dee is nearly hit by the car?

____

____

4 What mood do you think is created in this poem? Circle the answer you think is most correct.

cheerful excited miserable tense furious

5 What do you think Sinclair means when he writes that Dee is 'desperate to be an ordinary part of the night'?

____

____

Novel study: Runt

In Craig Silvey's novel *Runt*, a young girl and her family live in the drought-stricken town of Upson Downs. The farming community struggles against the weather and the greedy actions of the water-hoarding villain, Earl Robert-Barren. Annie and her talented dog, Runt, undertake several adventures, including performing in the Krumpets International Dog Show in London, in an effort to save her family's farm.

In this unit you will learn:

- how characters and settings are constructed
- how themes are developed through characters and conflicts
- the difference between types of narrative point of view
- how to write a book review.

Curriculum content

Australian Curriculum content description	Content code
Recognise language used to evaluate texts including visual and multimodal texts, and how evaluations of a text can be substantiated by reference to the text and other sources.	AC9E7LA02
Identify and describe how texts are structured differently depending on their purpose and how language features vary in texts.	AC9E7LA03
Explain the ways that literary devices and language features such as dialogue, and images are used to create character, and to influence emotions and opinions in different types of texts.	AC9E7LE03
Discuss the aesthetic and social value of literary texts using relevant and appropriate metalanguage.	AC9E7LE04
Identify and explain the ways that characters, settings and events combine to create meaning in narratives.	AC9E7LE05
Create and edit literary texts that experiment with language features and literary devices encountered in texts.	AC9E7LE07

Characters and characterisation

Every novel needs characters. These are the people (or animals or other beings) who populate the story. The main character is referred to as the **protagonist**. Read this extract from *Runt* in which we meet Annie, the protagonist.

protagonist The main character in a text

Annie Shearer lives in the town of Upson Downs.

She is eleven years old and short for her age. She has brown hair and brown eyes.

She lives on a sheep farm with her parents, Bryan and Susie, her brother Max and her grandma Dolly.

People in Upson Downs think Annie is a bit different.

They think it's odd that they have never seen her laugh, even though she is often quite happy.

They think it's strange that they've never seen her cry, even though she is sometimes quite sad.

They think it's weird that she wears an old leather tool belt wherever she goes, even though Annie finds it useful having so many pockets to store items that can be used to fix things.

They worry that she must be lonely because she spends so much time by herself. But Annie quite enjoys her own company—and besides, she has a very special friend.

He is a dog.

And his name is Runt.

Annie knows she is a bit different, but she doesn't think she is odd or strange or weird. The truth is, everybody is unique. No two people are the same. Even identical twins can have different interests. And it makes the world a more interesting place.

8.1 Check for understanding

1 Circle the words below that describe the character of Annie.

mature	different	friendly	lonely
adult	angry	clever	independent
humorous	caring	tall	

2 Highlight the words in the extract above that reveal how people in Upson Downs see Annie.

3 How is Annie's understanding of herself different from how others see her?

4 What is meant by the word 'runt'?

5 What does it suggest about Annie's character that she has a runt as a special friend?

We learn about characters by making inferences, or piecing together clues in the text. Sometimes the narrator will simply share character details, such as aspects of their personality or what they look like, but at other times we make inferences based on a character's actions and dialogue, as well as how others react to them.

Read this extract from *Runt* introducing the character of Max, Annie's brother.

Annie has a particular affection for honey badgers because they remind her of Max, her brother.

Max is thirteen years old. Like the honey badger, he has a sweet tooth. And above all else, Max Shearer is utterly fearless.

His dream is to be a famous daredevil. He films and edits his own videos for his YouTube channel, where you can see him perform such exploits as rolling down a hill inside an old tractor tyre, picking up a venomous snake, exploring an abandoned building that is rumoured to be haunted, holding his breath while submerged in a murky water trough, and riding a cranky ram like a rodeo cowboy.

Sadly, his efforts haven't yet propelled him to global notoriety. So with each new video, his stunts have become more elaborate and dangerous.

...

He wears a bright orange helmet from the 1980s, a pair of aviator sunglasses that cover half his face, and a dark green tracksuit with white stripes. He poses with a silver BMX bicycle and speaks enthusiastically to a camera propped on a post.

'G'day, viewers, it's Max Shearer here from *To the Max*, bringing you another wild stunt from Down Under. Today I'm taking it up a few notches. This one's called Rings of Fire. I'm gonna light up the tyres of my bike, pop a wheelie, fang it up this ramp here, do a wicked flip over this fence, and stick the landing. It's probably gonna be my most viral video ever. So, yeah. Um, thanks for spreading the word. Got my twenty-fifth subscriber during the week, so, pretty happy with that. Remember to chuck us a like and a comment. So, yeah. Let's get on with it!'

8.2 Check for understanding

1 Complete the following table describing the character of Max using information in the extract.

Aspect of characterisation	What we learn about Max	Is this information stated or inferred?
appearance		
actions		
dialogue		

2 In your own words, explain your interpretation of Max's character.

3 Think of a character from your favourite book or television show. What do you learn about them from their appearance, actions and dialogue?

Setting

'Setting' refers to the time and location in which a story takes place. In *Runt*, the story mainly takes place in Upson Downs, an Australian country town. Read this extract from *Runt* in which we find out information about Upson Downs.

Bryan drives through the main street of Upson Downs.

They pass empty storefronts with window banners that say FOR SALE or FOR LEASE. They pass Patel's Petals, the florist. Raelene's Relics, the antique store. They pass the bank, the butcher and the newsagent. They pass the Golden Fleece, the only pub left in town. They pass the abandoned town hall and the deserted railway station. They pass the Big Ram, a giant statue fallen into disrepair. It has a broken horn and a missing eye. The sign beneath it says THANK EWE FOR VISITING!

But nobody visits anymore.

For more than a hundred years, Upson Downs was busy and thriving. Home to thousands of people and thousands more sheep, Upson Downs was famous for producing the finest wool in the world. The luxurious fleece was praised by Parisian designers and prized by tailors on London's Savile Row.

The vast plains and valleys were kept green by the deep rivers and creeks that ran through it. It was a beautiful, vibrant place, full of wildlife and wildflowers. There were restaurants and festivals and dance halls and sporting clubs. There were stockyards and bake sales and charity events. People poured in from all across the country, and Upson Downs welcomed them all.

Then everything was ruined by one man.

8.3 Check for understanding

1 Circle the words in the following list that best describe the setting of Upson Downs as it is now.

vibrant	sad	quiet	productive
run-down	empty	bustling	lush
historic	changed		

2 The author, Craig Silvey, uses descriptive language to contrast the setting of Upson Downs before 'everything was ruined' with how it is now. In the extract above, highlight in one colour the words that describe Upson Downs in the past. Highlight in another colour the words that describe Upson Downs in the present.

3 What effect is created by juxtaposing, or placing side by side, these two contrasting descriptions?

____

____

____

____

4 Which words below best describe the mood, or feeling, established by the description of Upson Downs today?

a optimistic and upbeat ☐

b sad and gloomy ☐

c angry and threatening ☐

5 Craig Silvey uses a lot of visual description. In addition to visual details, writers often use other senses to help build the description of a setting. Write additional sentences below that use each of the following senses to help build a picture of Upson Downs in both the past and the present.

a smell

Past: ______________________________

Present: ______________________________

b sound

Past: ______________________________

Present: ______________________________

Plot and conflict

The 'plot' of a novel refers to the series of events that take place. Most novels follow a similar basic sequence of events:

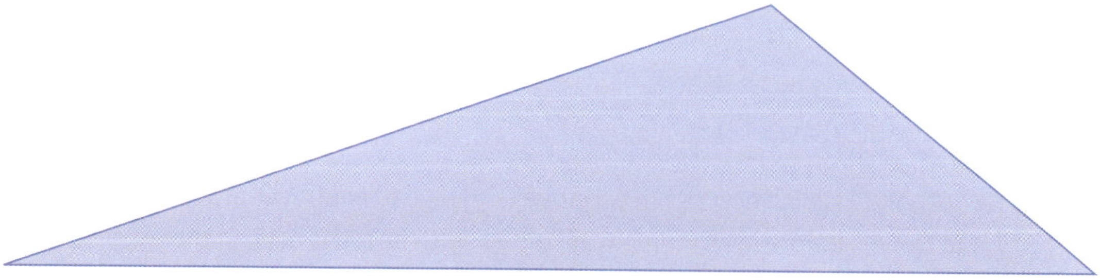

the beginning
(orientation or exposition)

The characters and setting are introduced, and a problem or conflict is established.

the middle
(rising action and climax)

The conflict grows through a series of events until the climax or high point of the story.

the ending
(resolution)

The conflict is resolved.

The plot is driven by conflict, or the problems faced by characters. There are three main types of conflict:

- *interpersonal*: conflict between characters
- *internal*: conflict within characters, such as a mental or moral struggle
- *external*: conflict between characters and their world, such as with nature or society.

In *Runt*, the character of Earl Robert-Barren has built a dam on his property to stop water flowing onto other people's farms. This causes a number of conflicts in the novel. Here is an example in the next extract.

Earl takes a seat behind a big oak desk. The shelf nearby features the sculpted busts of Earl's ancestors, each wearing their own white, curly-haired barrister's wig. Six generations of Robert-Barrens, stern and humourless and cold.

One entire wall is filled with fat leather-bound books about law. Contract law, family law, international law, privacy law, water law, agricultural law, tax law, criminal law, even laws *about* law.

But Bryan's attention is drawn to an easel holding a map of Upson Downs. It shows the boundary lines of every farm in the district. Earl has marked in green every property he now owns.

Bryan's stomach drops with dread when he sees his own farm on the map, surrounded by blocks of green.

Earl clicks his fingers to get Bryan's attention.

'Mr Shearer, any further recurrences would not be handled so charitably. The next time your sheep wander onto my land, I'll be issuing a writ of ownership. Not that I particularly want them. They are a sorry-looking herd, I must say. Skinny as greyhounds. Your father would be ashamed of their condition. He had a sterling reputation for raising quality fleece; it's a shame to see it sullied. Still, the whole town seems to be in decline these days. It's a pity.'

Bryan flashes with anger.

'You're right, Earl. A lot of us *are* in decline. Might have something to do with the fact that you stole our water.'

'*Stole?* What is on *my* property is *mine* to keep—including your sheep, should they trespass again. My actions are perfectly aboveboard. I have always acted in strict accordance with the law. You're welcome to pursue legal action should you suspect otherwise.'

'As you well know, Earl, my father tried that for years, but you delayed and adjourned and counter-sued and used every dirty trick until we ran out of money.'

Earl leans back in his chair.

'If your financial position is dire, Mr Shearer, I'd be willing to make a fair offer on your property.'

8.4 Check for understanding

1 Find definitions for the following words.

a writ ______

b sterling ______

c sullied ______

d accordance ______

e adjourned ______

f dire ______

2 What has Earl been doing to the farms in Upson Downs?

______

______

3 Use the internet to find out what is meant by the following terms.

a earl ______

b robber baron ______

4 How does the author use Earl's name to suggest his character?

______

______

5 Why do you think Bryan's stomach 'drops with dread' when he sees the map?

______

______

6 As a farmer and a father, what internal conflict do you think Bryan is experiencing?

______

______

7 Give an example of each of the following conflicts evident in this passage.

a interpersonal ______

b external ______

8 Think of a novel you have read before. Fill in the table, identifying examples of each type of conflict found in that book.

Internal	
Interpersonal	
External	

Thinking about themes

Themes are the 'big ideas' explored in a story. Most authors won't just tell you the themes directly; readers have to work out the 'big ideas' behind the story themselves. One way to do this is to look at what the characters go through and think about what you can learn from their experiences. Here are some common themes found in literature.

> **theme** The main idea, concept or message of a text

fate/destiny	courage	freedom	greed
choice	family	love	the underdog
power	good versus evil	loyalty	overcoming challenges
sacrifice	friendship		

8.5 Reflecting and discussing

Discuss the following questions in pairs, in small groups or with the whole class, as directed by your teacher.

1 Based on the extracts you have read from *Runt*, which themes from the above list do you think it might explore? Why?

2 Why do you think so many books and films explore similar themes? Why are people interested in these 'big ideas'?

8.6 Get creative

Both Annie and her dog, Runt, are underdogs. This means they are underestimated by others and seem unlikely to succeed.

1 Create your own underdog character. Write a few sentences here briefly describing your character. What makes this character an underdog?

____

____

____

2 In your notebook, write a short story about your underdog character following the typical plot sequence above.

Language features

Authors use a variety of language features, including descriptive and figurative language, to make their stories interesting and to bring their themes to life. Read the following extract from *Runt* and notice the use of highly effective language features.

> Runt was as slippery as an eel and cunning as a fox. He could dart like a rabbit, bounce like a gazelle and climb like a monkey. He was spry and agile and clever. Constable Bayleaf would sprint after him, wielding a long pole with a rope snare at the end, but Runt would dodge and weave and feint. He would leap over cars, crawl under fences and scale walls with ease.
>
> People in the street would often join in the chase, trying to snatch him and dive on him and trap him, but Runt slipped past them all, vanishing into the shadows like a panther in the jungle, leaving behind a parade of panting pedestrians and one thwarted constable.

8.7 Check for understanding

Descriptive language

1 Find definitions for the following adjectives.

a cunning ________________________________

b spry ________________________________

c agile ________________________________

2 Descriptive detail can also be added by choosing specific verbs. Draw lines to match the verbs below with their definitions.

wield	a sudden move intended to distract
feint	to block or frustrate someone
thwart	to use effectively

3 Identify three other verbs used to describe Runt's movements as he is being chased.

____

4 Use a dictionary or thesaurus to find more specific verbs to replace the following actions.

a cry ____

b run ____

c speak ____

d smile ____

Figurative language

5 **Similes** offer a comparison between two things, often using 'like' or 'as'. Highlight six similes in the passage above that are used to describe Runt.

6 **Metaphors** offer a comparison between two things by suggesting that one thing is another. What picture is created in your mind by the metaphor of a 'a parade of panting pedestrians'?

____

____

7 Connotations are associations we make with a particular word or phrase. Circle the qualities you associate with the word 'runt'.

small	large
aggressive	timid
meek	assertive
strong	weak

8 What is the overall picture created of Runt in the extract?

____

____

____

simile A device comparing 2 things that are not alike. Similes use 'like', 'as' or 'than' to make the comparison (e.g. The cake was as light as air)
metaphor A type of figurative language used to describe a person or object through an implicit comparison to something with similar characteristics

Narrative point of view

Narrative **point of view** refers to the perspective from which a story is told. This may be the perspective of a character within the story or of an external observer. There are four main narrative points of view:

First person	Second person
The story is told from the perspective of a character using the pronoun 'I'. e.g. I set out from the cabin, following a path I could see twisting its way through the forest.	Less commonly used, the story is told as if you, the reader, are a character in the story. It uses the pronoun 'you'. e.g. Along the way, you could hear the eerie cackle of a kookaburra and a rustling in the scrub that seemed to follow your every step.
Third person (limited)	**Third person (omniscient)**
The story is told by an external narrator who has access to the thoughts and feelings of one character. e.g. Jo shivered, the sun shielded by the dense canopy of the forest. She was worried she would lose sight of her dad as his checked shirt disappeared around a bend.	The story is told by an all-knowing external narrator who has access to the thoughts and feelings of all characters. e.g. Jo quickened her step, eager to catch up. Her dad turned around, wondering why she was dawdling so far behind.

Runt is told from the third-person omniscient point of view. The reader gets to experience the thoughts and feelings of several characters. For example, after Max attempts his Rings of Fire stunt, we read the following passage.

point of view The position from which the text is designed to be perceived (e.g. a narrator might take a role of first or third person, omniscient or restricted in knowledge of events or the opinion presented in a text)

At that same moment, propelled by an instinct for her son's stupidity, or the smell of smouldering rubber, or both, Susie Shearer steps out of the house. She scans the surroundings suspiciously, and sees that her son's pants have just caught fire.

We only know what has motivated Max's mum because the omniscient narrator is able to tell us that she was 'propelled by an instinct for her son's stupidity, or the smell of smouldering rubber'.

8.8 Reflecting and discussing

Discuss the following questions in pairs, in small groups or with the whole class, as directed by your teacher.

1 How different do you think the story would be if told by Annie in the first person?

2 What advantages and disadvantages might come from using a first-person narrative point of view?

Punctuating dialogue

Dialogue, or direct speech, is an important part of many novels. The reader can learn a lot about characters from their dialogue. Dialogue also helps the plot move forward by communicating events and conflicts. Including dialogue in a story requires very specific punctuation.

dialogue

dialogue goes inside inverted commas or speech marks

speech tags can come before, in the middle of or after dialogue

a comma is used to separate dialogue from the speech tag

'Why are you all drenched?' asks Bryan.

'It's *raining*!' they yell at once.

'What?'

'It worked, Annie!' says Max. 'The Rainmaker worked! You made a whole storm!'

Bryan looks at Annie.

'What is he talking about?'

'Is it really raining?' Annie asks. 'Or is this a Kind Lie?'

'It's smashing down!' says Dolly. 'Never seen anything like it. 'The water tank's full already!'

'The whole district has been soaked,' says Susie. 'It's a miracle!'

speech tag

punctuation goes inside the speech marks

dialogue is broken up with action

not every piece of dialogue needs a speech tag if it is clear who is speaking

a new line is used for each new speaker

dialogue starts with a capital letter

8.9 Check for understanding

1 Add correct punctuation and capitalisation to the following sentences.

a What's for dinner, Mum? I yelled I'm starving.

b It's just the wind Millie whispered to herself, suddenly afraid.

c That was close Harry said as the car sped past him.

d Ava asked can you tell me where the bus stop is?

2 Write a short section of imagined dialogue between two friends arguing over a misunderstanding.

____

____

____

____

____

____

____

____

Book reviews

People write reviews to share their opinions about the quality of books and other texts, and to recommend them to other people – or not! Reviews are published in newspapers, magazines and online, and sometimes in video form. Read the review of *Runt.*

Scan the QR code, or click here to access the review.

Knowing the news

In the past, the main way to 'get the news' was to read a newspaper. Today, there are many ways to find out what is happening around us: we can listen to the radio, watch television, read online articles, follow social media sites or use apps on our phones. How do you and your family find out about what is going on in the world?

In this unit you will learn:

- about the features of a newspaper article
- how to compare different online news articles
- how to use colons, brackets and dashes to support meaning
- whether printed newspapers are still valuable or not.

Curriculum content

Australian Curriculum content description	Content code
Understand that the cohesion of texts relies on devices that signal structure and guide readers, such as overviews and initial and concluding paragraphs.	AC9E7LA04
Understand the use of punctuation including colons and brackets to support meaning.	AC9E7LA09
Explain the effect of current technology on reading, creating and responding to texts including media texts.	AC9E7LY01

What is the news?

'The news' refers to information about people, events and issues that are considered 'newsworthy' or important for people to be informed about.

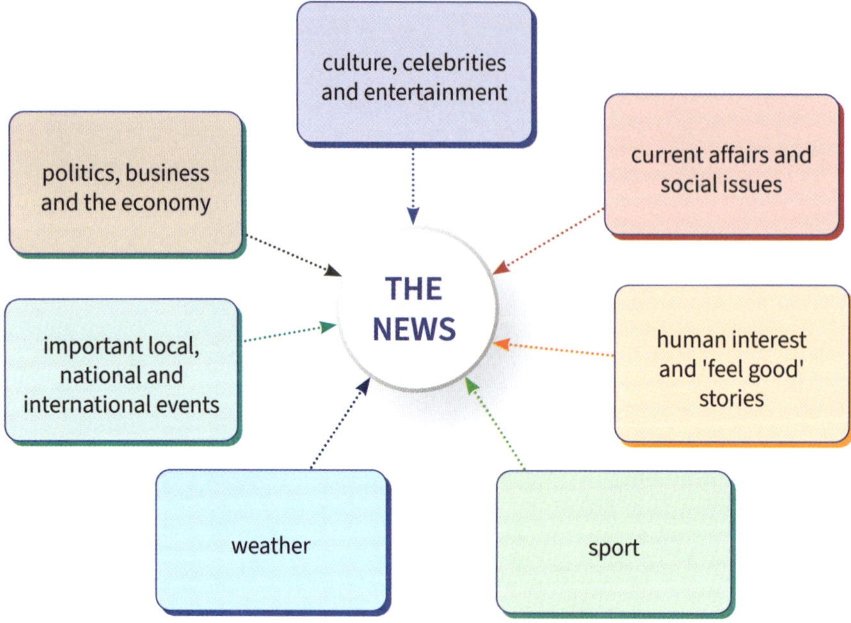

9.1 Reflecting and discussing

Discuss the following questions in pairs, in small groups or with the whole class, as directed by your teacher.

1. What items above are you most interested in being kept informed about?
2. How do you learn about the news – do you read a printed or online newspaper, watch it on television, hear it on the radio, or stream it through social media? What sources do your parents or grandparents use? Make a tally of your answers within your class or group.

Read the following newspaper article.

ISSUE 1 NEWSPAPER NEWS

Plastic's Worst Nightmare: Fungi Found to be Potent Predator

Eric Mann, 1 May 2023

Scientists have developed a new strain of fungi that can break down plastic, offering a potential solution to the global issue of plastic waste management.

Australian researchers at the University of Sydney had been experimenting with the fungus, known as *Aspergillus terreus,* when they discovered its unusual properties. Naturally found in the Amazon rainforest, the strain has shown the ability to consume plastic in a matter of weeks, a process that would typically take hundreds of years to occur naturally.

The research team tested the fungus on different types of plastic, including polypropylene, which is found in many common products: takeaway containers, disposable cutlery, and cling film. The fungus was able to break down the plastic by producing enzymes that dissolve the chemical bonds of the material, allowing it to be consumed as food.

The lead on the project, Professor Ali Abbas, was excited by the potential of the fungus's ability to break down plastic.

This fungus, a type of mould really, 'has the highest degradation rate reported in the literature that we know in the world,' the professor said.

In Australia alone, more than 13,000 tonnes of polypropylene-based plastics are dumped into landfill every year – either because consumers choose not to recycle or because it is contaminated with foodstuffs and other non-recyclable materials.

'This [the discovery of the fungus] is incredibly exciting because plastic is such a big environmental challenge,' explained Dr Ilia Leitch, a plant scientist at Kew Gardens in London.

'If this can be the solution to a problem the world doesn't know how to fix – a problem that is destroying our oceans – then that would be absolutely wonderful.'

However, experts have cautioned that the process of using the fungus on a large scale is still in its early stages and requires further research. 'Despite the massive scale of plastic production and consumption, there has been very little attention paid to plastics degradation under environmental conditions, and our understanding of how plastics can be degraded is limited,' explained Professor Abbas.

There are also the added issues of limited funding for, and declining interest in, fungi research. As noted by Dr Leitch, 'It's tricky sometimes to sell them [fungi]. But maybe we can do it by making people realize the potential role of fungi in beating these environmental challenges.'

Despite these limitations, the possibility of the fungus as a solution to plastic waste management has generated excitement among scientists and environmentalists.

9.2 Check for understanding

1 Tick the sentences below that express the main points of the article.

a The plastic-eating fungus may help with the recycling crisis. ☐

b Mould can be dangerous for human health. ☐

c Scientists have discovered a plastic-eating fungus. ☐

d Australia has a strong recycling program for plastics. ☐

e A new type of fungus was discovered in the Amazon rainforest. ☐

2 Why do you think this scientific discovery is considered newsworthy?

____

____

____

Features of news articles

News articles follow a basic structure and are usually written in a particular **style**.

Headlines

A headline uses a limited number of words and needs to be factually correct, attract attention and suggest what the article is about. Headlines can use different techniques and tones to make you want to read the article. Some techniques include emotive language, puns and alliteration.

Headline tone	Example
sensationalist (overhyped)	Holiday hell! Mouse plague overruns resort
factual (matter of fact)	Police search for witnesses after fatal crash
humorous (amusing)	Geelong Cats barely scratch opposition
clickbait (to attract curiosity)	Why ChatGPT might actually be good for homework

style The distinctive language features, text structures and/or subject matter in a text which may shape meaning, be enjoyed for its aesthetic qualities or distinguish the work of an author, period etc

Other structural elements

By-line

The by-line gives the writer's name and sometimes other details like their location or job title. In online articles, the by-line usually includes the date.

Lead

The lead is the very first sentence of a news article. It should clearly communicate the essential facts of the story in a concise statement.

Graphics

If the article includes a graphic, such as a photo or diagram, it will be eye-catching and help to illustrate what the article is saying.

Pull quotes

Sometimes, important quotes are pulled from the main text and enlarged or made to stand out in some other way to draw attention to them.

Main paragraphs

The main paragraphs will cover the 'who', 'what', 'when', 'why' and 'how' of the topic, usually in an 'inverted pyramid' format. This means the most important information is included first, with each successive paragraph including details of lower importance ('inverted' means 'upside down').

This structure is used for two reasons.

First, readers may not be interested in reading a lot about the topic and may only want to read the first couple of sentences, so the most important information should be there.

Second, if editors need to shorten news stories quickly, they just cut paragraphs from the bottom.

Journalistic style

News articles have particular ways of using language (or 'style' of language). News articles:

- » use sources, facts, statistics and quotes from experts or witnesses
- » should be objective, meaning they don't show the writer's opinion (this is different from opinion pieces, which are subjective)
- » are tightly written with no unnecessary words
- » use short paragraphs of only one or two sentences
- » are written in the active voice ('Scientists have discovered …') instead of the passive voice ('A discovery was made by scientists …').

9.3 Check for understanding

1 Annotate the news article about the plastic-eating fungi according to the following instructions.

a Underline the headline.

b Put an asterisk (*) beside the by-line.

c Highlight the lead sentence in one colour.

d Highlight an example of a quote from an expert or witness in another colour.

e Cross out the paragraphs you would delete if you had to cut 60 words from the article.

2 Draw lines to match each of the headlines below with the correct article summary.

Headline	Article summary
Taxi murder could be random, cops say	Melbourne's outer suburbs are seeing more auctions than ever, boosting house prices on the city's edges.
Hammer time in outer Melbourne	Some Australian fashion brands are taking big steps to stamp out exploitation of workers from their supply chains.
How to avoid slavery in your fashion	Police have issued a statement that the fatal attack on a taxi driver in Hobart is likely to have been unprovoked.

3 Use these article summaries to construct short and effective headlines.

a Melbourne has just been named the sporting capital city of the world.

____

b The government is considering a limit on tourists visiting the Great Barrier Reef.

____

c A plane carrying Ukrainian refugees has landed at Sydney Airport.

____

4 Number the paragraphs below to make them fit the journalistic 'inverted pyramid' format, with 1 being the most important information and 4 being the least important.

Ancient mega whale remains discovered

☐ The finder of the tooth was keen fossil fossicker Murray Orr. 'When you find something that is special, you know it,' Mr Orr said.

☐ A fossilised whale tooth has been found on a suburban beach, a world-renowned fossil site. A spokesperson for Museum Victoria says it is an internationally significant find, as it represents the first evidence of this species of sperm whale outside the Americas.

☐ The marine giant's size is estimated at 18 metres long and its weight as 40,000 kilograms, based on the 30-centimetre, 3-kilogram tooth. It is the largest whale tooth ever collected in Australia.

☐ The tooth hails from the Pliocene epoch, making it approximately 5 million years old. The tooth of this whale reveals it was a fearsome predator that would have hunted other whales.

Colons, brackets and dashes

Colons, brackets and dashes can be used to add clarifying detail to a sentence.

Colons draw attention to the information that follows. They can introduce a list, a subtitle, an example or an independent but related clause. For example:

» Reef Revelations: Amazing facts about Australia's coral reef systems

» Australia has many coral reefs popular with tourists: the Great Barrier Reef, Ningaloo Reef and the Gove Peninsula.

» The reefs are delicate ecosystems: sustainable tourism is essential for their survival.

» Reef tourists should heed one simple rule: look, but don't touch.

Brackets (also known as parentheses) are used to provide additional explanatory detail – just as they do in this sentence! The sentence must still make sense if the bracketed information is removed. For example:

» The Great Barrier Reef was recognised as a World Heritage Area by UNESCO (United Nations Educational, Scientific and Cultural Organization) in 1981.

» Many reefs are in danger of bleaching events (when stressed corals expel the algae that give them colour) as a result of rising sea temperatures.

» For Amy Gash (a custodian of Lady Elliot Island), sustainable tourism is important in ensuring the conservation of the reef.

Dashes are used in a similar way to brackets – to add clarifying or additional detail. For example:

» Victoria is home to a lesser-known – but equally important – reef system known as the Great Southern Reef.

» The Great Southern Reef is composed of thousands of kilometres of rocky outcrops teeming with marine life – unlike the coral at the heart of the Great Barrier Reef.

» Species inhabiting the Great Southern Reef are at risk because of its location in a hotspot – where sea temperatures are rising rapidly – and along a heavily populated coastline.

9.4

Check for understanding

1 Add a colon to each of the following sentences if and where appropriate.

a Looking at the reef, Jason could only think of one word wow!

b Reefs are home to diverse marine life crabs, corals, sponges, sea urchins and many species of fish.

c Sustainable tourism can help save Australia's reefs.

2 Put brackets around the clarifying detail in these sentences.

a The DCCEEW Department of Climate Change, Energy, the Environment and Water is the Australian Government's environmental protection agency.

b We spoke to Ana Singh a tour guide in Victoria about a trip to Heron Island.

3 Tick the examples below where dashes have been used correctly.

a In 2019, concrete pyramids were sunk off the coast of Darwin – the capital city of the Northern Territory – to create an artificial reef. ☐

b These concrete pyramids will encourage an entire reef system – to develop over time. ☐

c This artificial reef system has been used elsewhere – including Port Macquarie and Hervey Bay – with great success. ☐

d Since they were put in place – over one hundred species have been sighted – and more are expected to come. ☐

Comparing online news articles

Today, many people are choosing to access news online. The digital format allows news sites to include features that are not possible in print formats such as newspapers or magazines.

9.5 Reflecting and discussing

Discuss the following questions in pairs, in small groups or with the whole class, as directed by your teacher.

1. Compared with printed news articles, what additional features do you imagine online news sites can include within their articles?
2. What other benefits come from publishing news online rather than in a traditional newspaper?
3. What reasons can you give for why some people prefer accessing news online?

9.6 Check for understanding

Look at two online news sites, such as *news.com.au*, *The Age, The Guardian Australia edition, The Saturday Paper* or *The Sydney Morning Herald*. Fill in the following table, identifying the features typical of online news sites. (Note that the first screen that opens up when you go to a website is known as the 'splash page'.)

Features to identify	News site 1	News site 2
Describe the masthead (the banner at the top of the page), including the title, crest, slogan and date.		
Does the splash page use a grid layout for the various articles?		
Do most articles on the splash page include only a headline and lead? Do you have to click through to read the rest of the article?		
Are there drop-down menus allowing access to different sections or types of news? List these sections.		
Does the site include lots of images and videos? Are these in colour or black and white?		

UNIT 10

Explain it to me

We use informative and instructional texts almost every day. We find information online and in books or guides, and we follow instructions to learn how to do just about anything, whether building a treehouse, constructing a piece of furniture or cooking spaghetti bolognaise. Instructional texts are often called 'procedural texts'. Without these important types of texts, we would find it very hard to learn about anything!

In this unit you will learn:

- the ways in which informative and procedural texts are structured
- how connectives can create cohesion in texts
- how to use complex and compound sentences to add detail.

Curriculum content

Australian Curriculum content description	Content code
Understand how complex and compound-complex sentences can be used to elaborate, extend and explain ideas.	AC9E7LA05
Analyse the ways in which language features shape meaning and vary according to audience and purpose.	AC9E7LY03
Explain the structure of ideas such as the use of taxonomies, cause and effect, extended metaphors and chronology.	AC9E7LY04

Types of informative and procedural texts

There are many types of informative and procedural texts. Some examples of these texts are listed below.

Informative	Procedural
reports	recipes
websites	how-to guides
essays	user manuals
encyclopedias	safety procedures
textbooks	assembly instructions
brochures	travel directions
historical accounts	maintenance procedures
fact sheets	product usage guides
infographics	tutorials

10.1 Reflecting and discussing

Discuss the following questions in pairs, in small groups or with the whole class, as directed by your teacher.

1 What sorts of informative texts do you use every day?

2 What sorts of procedural texts have you followed?

3 Apart from written texts, what other sorts of informative and procedural texts do people often use today? For example, do you look for online tutorials or videos?

Informative texts

Read the following extract from an informative text on pets.

Swimming Through Time:
The Fascinating History of Pet Goldfish

Goldfish are one of the most popular and beloved pets in the world. These small, colourful fish are a common sight in pet stores and aquariums, but where did they come from? And how did they end up in a bowl in your living room? Their origins can be traced back to ancient China.

History of pet goldfish

The exact date of the domestication of goldfish is not known, but it is believed to have occurred over 1,000 years ago during the Tang Dynasty in China (618–907 CE). They were treasured for their beauty, and many varieties were developed, including the 'dragon eyes' goldfish with protruding eyes and the 'lionhead' goldfish with its mane-like growth.

During the Ming Dynasty (1368–1644), goldfish became popular among the wealthy and were kept in elaborate ponds and water gardens. They were often given as gifts to the imperial court and other important figures. The popularity of goldfish as pets continued to grow, and by the Qing Dynasty (1644–1911), they were widely kept in home aquariums.

In the nineteenth century, goldfish were introduced to Europe and North America, where they quickly became popular pets. Goldfish breeding became a hobby for a new generation, and many more varieties were developed, including the iconic 'comet' and 'shubunkin' goldfish.

Breeding attractive pets

Goldfish were originally bred from a species of wild carp called the Prussian carp. Since the Tang Dynasty, fish breeders have used their understanding of genetics to produce a number of variations through centuries of selective breeding. These variations have made goldfish attractive pets.

Some of these variations include:

- ***bright colours***: colours such as red, orange, yellow, white and black
- ***unique shapes***: variations include round, egg-shaped and slender-bodied
- ***fin shape***: from long and flowing to short and rounded
- ***scale type***: scales may have metallic, pearl or matte appearances
- ***eye size***: some varieties have protruding or enlarged eyes
- ***disease resistance***: hardy breeds make goldfish easier to care for.

Today, goldfish are one of the most popular species of fish kept as pets worldwide. In China, goldfish are thought to bring good luck and prosperity, but people everywhere appreciate these cute little fish. They are hardy and easy to care for, and come in a wide variety of colours and patterns. Next time you see a goldfish, know that its ancestors have been appreciated for over a thousand years!

DID YOU KNOW?

The scientific name for the common goldfish is *Carassius auratus*. *Auratus* comes from the Latin word for gold: *aurum*.

FUN FACT!

Despite popular belief, goldfish have a remarkable memory and can remember things for up to several months. They can even learn to recognise the faces of their owners or to perform tricks!

10.2 Check for understanding

1 Look up definitions for the following words:

a beloved ______

b domestication ______

c dynasty ______

d protruding ______

e iconic ______

f prosperity ______

2 Why did goldfish become popular in ancient China?

______

3 Identify two variations that have been bred into goldfish.

______

4 Identify three reasons why goldfish are popular pets today.

______

5 What is the purpose of this text? Select the best answer below.

a to argue why goldfish make good pets ☐

b to explain how goldfish came to be pets ☐

c to persuade people to breed goldfish ☐

d to tell a story about goldfish in ancient China ☐

6 Identify three features of this text that help readers find information quickly.

______

______

______

7 How would you describe the language used in this text? Circle three words below.

chatty	humorous	factual	descriptive
casual	poetic	critical	figurative
opinionated	clear		

Conventions of informative texts

Informative text structures

Informative texts are structured in clear and logical ways. They use headings, subheadings and other features such as tables of contents and indexes in order to clearly signpost different parts of the text. In addition, graphics and diagrams can be used to help illustrate and clarify written information.

The information included is also sequenced in ways that help guide the reader from one idea to the next in a logical fashion. Depending on the type of information, there are several ways to structure an informative text.

Description or classification	Sequence	Cause and effect	Compare/contrast	Problem and solution
» Texts that use this structure describe or provide information about the topic. » They begin with a general explanation and then organise or classify further information into subtopics.	» Texts that use this structure organise information into a logical sequence. » Sequences might be arranged by chronology (time order), steps in a procedure or order of importance.	» Texts that use this structure explore the causes and effects of events, issues or conflicts. » They begin with an overview of the topic and then explore the causes followed by the effects or outcomes.	» Texts that use this structure show the similarities and differences between two or more things. » They begin by introducing the things to be compared, and then indicate ways they are similar or different.	» Texts that use this structure explore ways that problems, issues or conflicts might be resolved. » They begin by outlining a problem and identifying who it affects before explaining possible solutions.

Informative text style

- *Clear and concise language:* the language is easy to follow and understand.
- *Objective tone:* information is presented without bias or personal opinion.
- *Technical vocabulary:* technical terms may be used but are clearly defined for the reader.
- *Evidence*: evidence and examples are included to support information presented in the text.
- *Active voice*: the active voice is used to clearly identify the subject of each sentence.
- *Connectives*: connective language is used to create a coherent flow of information.

Complex and compound-complex sentences

Informative texts often use sophisticated sentence structures to explain and elaborate on their ideas. **Complex** and compound-complex sentences are types of sentences that are made up of more than one clause.

A **clause** is a group of words that contains a **subject** and a **verb**.

complex sentence A sentence with one or more subordinate clauses. In the following example, the subordinate clause is shown in brackets: I took my umbrella [because it was raining]
clause A grammatical unit referring to a happening or state e.g. 'the team won' (happening), 'the dog is red' (state), usually containing a subject and a verb group/phrase
subject A word or group of words (usually a noun group/phrase) in a sentence or clause representing the person, thing or idea doing the action that follows (e.g. 'The dog [subject] was barking')
verb A word class that expresses processes that include doing, feeling, thinking, saying and relating

A complex sentence has one *independent clause* and one or more *dependent clauses*. The independent clause can stand alone as a sentence, but the dependent clause cannot. Dependent clauses often begin with words like 'although', 'since', 'because', 'which' and 'while', especially if they are at the beginning of sentences.

If a dependent clause begins a sentence, it usually needs a comma to separate it from the independent clause.

For example:

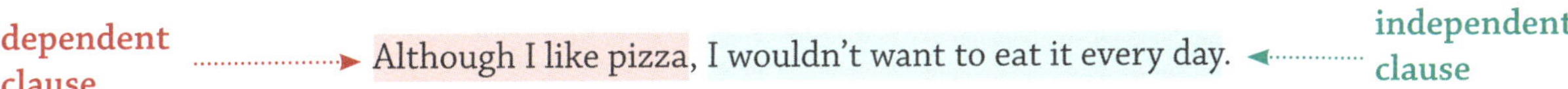

A compound-complex sentence has two or more independent clauses and one or more dependent clauses.

For example:

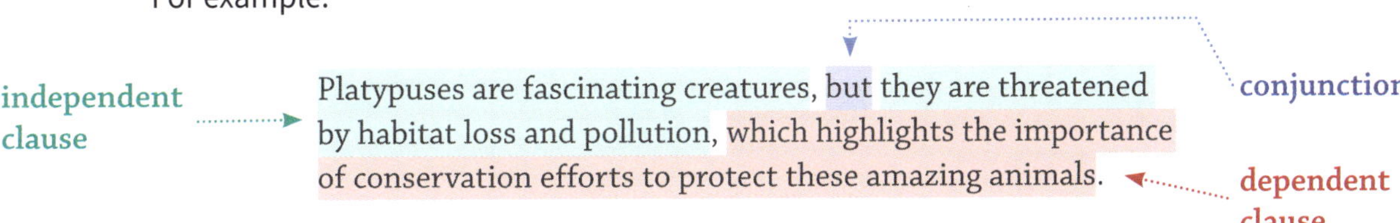

When writing complex and compound-complex sentences, it's important to pay attention to the punctuation and the conjunctions used to connect the clauses. By combining different clauses, we can add more detail to our ideas.

10.3 Check for understanding

1 Underline the independent clauses in the following complex sentences.
For example: When I finish my homework, <u>I will watch TV.</u>

a Computer games are a popular way to relax, although some argue that they can teach complex thinking skills.

b Because of its use in batteries, lithium has become an increasingly valuable export for Australia.

c Primarily nocturnal, echidnas are sometimes found foraging during the day.

d Self-driving cars are fast becoming reality, which may reduce the number of accidents on our roads.

e Although making ice-cream can be time-consuming, the end result is well worth the effort.

2 Rewrite the following simple sentences as complex sentences by adding a dependent clause to each.
Example:

Simple sentence: The dog barked.

Complex sentence: When the mailman arrived, the dog barked.

a The sun rose.

____

b The teacher finished the lesson.

____

c We cooked a barbecue.

____

d Maria dropped Sam off at school.

____

e The crowd roared.

____

3 Combine the following sentences to create a compound-complex sentence.
Example:

The birds were chirping. The sun was shining. I went for a walk.

Compound-complex sentence: The birds were chirping and the sun was shining, so I went for a walk.

a The students studied hard. They passed their Science test. They were very happy.

____

b The concert was sold out. I wanted to go. I couldn't get a ticket.

____

c Allie loves to dance. She practises every day. She hopes to be a professional dancer one day.

____

d The sun was setting. The sky turned orange. We knew it was time to head back home.

____

4 Identify whether the following sentences are simple, compound, complex or compound-complex.

a The dog barked and the cat ran away. ______________________

b Although it was raining, the concert continued. ______________________

c She is reading a book that her friend recommended. ______________________

d The coach was pleased with the team's efforts, but she thought they needed to train harder. ______________________

Procedural texts

Procedural texts are a special type of informative text that explain how to do something.

Scan the QR code or click here to access the following procedural text.

Connectives

Connectives are words that link paragraphs and sentences together in a logical way. They can show relationships of sequence, cause and effect, comparison or addition, or add emphasis. They are important for creating **cohesion** (unity) in texts.

connective Words linking, and logically relating ideas to one another, in paragraphs and sentences indicating relationships of time, cause and effect, comparison, addition, condition and concession or clarification
cohesion Grammatical or lexical relationships that bind different parts of a text together and give it unity. It is achieved through devices such as reference, substitution, repetition and text connectives

Type of connective	Examples
addition	also, furthermore, in addition
contrast	however, on the other hand, but
cause and effect	because, as a result, consequently
sequence	first, second, finally
comparison	similarly, likewise, in the same way
emphasis	indeed, in fact, certainly

10.4

Check for understanding

1 Look up definitions for the following words:

a maintenance ______

b thrive ______

c filtration ______

d aeration ______

e substrate ______

f beneficial ______

2 Why do you need to add some water before putting in plants and decorations?

______

3 What is the purpose of water conditioner?

______

4 What do you think 'aquascaping' means?

______

5 What is the purpose of this text? Select the best answer below.

a to tell a story about someone's experience with goldfish ☐

b to explain why substrate is important in goldfish bowls ☐

c to instruct someone on how to set up a healthy goldfish bowl ☐

d to persuade someone to keep goldfish as pets ☐

6 Look at the structure of the text.

a Why is a picture of the completed fishbowl included?

____

b Why is the equipment listed before the instructions?

____

____

c Why are the instructions numbered?

____

d What additional features might help readers to set up a goldfish bowl?

____

____

7 Does the language in the text make it appear easy or difficult to set up a goldfish bowl? Include two short examples from the text to support your answer.

____

____

8 Insert connectives in the gaps below to help with the cohesion of these sentences from a procedural text. Choose from the following words.

so	alternatively	in fact
secondly	because	finally

a ________________, add some water to the bowl.

b ________________, live plants are a great option ________________ they help to oxygenate the water and provide natural filtration.

c ________________ add your goldfish.

Using comprehension strategies

Every day, you will come across a range of texts that you will need to comprehend. To 'comprehend' something means to understand and make meaning from it. These texts that you are required to understand might include an advertisement on television, a recipe for dinner, a train timetable, an explanation in a textbook, a webpage, a chapter of a novel you're reading, or the feed on a social media site. Clearly, comprehension plays a vital role in all of our lives on a daily basis. Well-developed comprehension skills allow us to function easily rather than living in a state of complete confusion.

In this unit you will learn:

- about different comprehension strategies
- to practise using different comprehension strategies for a range of text forms
- to use comprehension strategies to enhance your understanding and enjoyment of texts.

Curriculum content

Australian Curriculum content description	Content code
Identify and describe how texts are structured differently depending on their purpose and how language features vary in texts.	AC9E7LA03
Use comprehension strategies such as visualising, predicting, connecting, summarising, monitoring, questioning and inferring to analyse and summarise information and ideas.	AC9E7LY05

What are comprehension strategies?

comprehension strategies Processes used by readers to make meaning from texts. They include activating and using prior knowledge, predicting likely future events in a text, monitoring meaning and critically reflecting

Comprehension strategies are the specific processes we use to make sense of texts so that we can understand them. This unit will particularly draw your attention to the following comprehension skills:

Each of these strategies is explained separately below. However, it is important to remember that often you will use more than one strategy at the same time to comprehend a text. Indeed, the **Check for understanding** and **Reflecting and discussing** activities throughout Units 1–10 of this book integrate a range of different comprehension strategies simultaneously.

In this unit, the comprehension strategies that are a particular focus in each section are indicated before the activities commence. This will help you to be aware of the specific processes you are using in each activity.

Summary of common comprehension strategies

Skimming is reading quickly in order to get a general overview of a text. It only allows for an overall impression of the text but is a very useful strategy in helping you decide what kind of text you are reading and identifying its main topic.

Scanning involves reading quickly in order to find specific facts, words or phrases. This strategy requires you to move your eyes quickly down the text to find only the information that will answer a particular question.

Activating prior knowledge requires you to think about what you already know to help you understand a new text. It may involve you brainstorming what you already know about a text's main topic or making connections with something similar you have already read.

Visualising involves forming a mental image or picture in your head to illustrate what you are reading.

Predicting involves making a logical presumption about what might happen next in a text, often based on prior experience of similar texts.

Connecting is about making links between the text you are trying to understand and other texts. It also involves thinking about how the text relates to you and to the world at large.

Summarising involves choosing only the most important information in a text and then rewriting it in shortened form.

Questioning refers to asking yourself questions before, during or after reading a text, in ways that help you think more deeply about what you are reading and help clarify your understanding.

Inferring means making a deduction about what something might mean. Even though a text might not state something specifically, you will be able to draw logical conclusions based on the clues or hints it offers and through your skills of reasoning.

Comprehension focus 1: skimming and scanning

The following text is an extract from *Harry Potter and the Philosopher's Stone* by J. K. Rowling.

Dudley's birthday – how could he have forgotten? Harry got slowly out of bed and started looking for socks. He found a pair under his bed and, after pulling a spider off one of them, put them on. Harry was used to spiders, because the cupboard under the stairs was full of them, and that was where he slept.

When he was dressed he went down the hall into the kitchen. The table was almost hidden beneath all Dudley's birthday presents. It looked as though Dudley had got the new computer he wanted, not to mention the second television and the racing bike. Exactly why Dudley wanted a racing bike was a mystery to Harry, as Dudley was very fat and hated exercise – unless of course it involved punching somebody. Dudley's favourite punch-bag was Harry, but he couldn't often catch him. Harry didn't look it, but he was very fast.

Perhaps it had something to do with living in a dark cupboard, but Harry had always been small and skinny for his age. He looked even smaller and skinnier than he really was because all he had to wear were old clothes of Dudley's and Dudley was about four times bigger than he was. Harry had a thin face, knobbly knees, black hair and bright-green eyes. He wore round glasses held together with a lot of Sellotape because of all the times Dudley had punched him on the nose. The only thing Harry liked about his own appearance was a very thin scar on his forehead which was shaped like a bolt of lightning. He had had it as long as he could remember and the first question he could ever remember asking his Aunt Petunia was how he had got it.

'In the car crash when your parents died,' she had said. 'And don't ask questions.'

11.1

Activity

1 **Skim** the extract and circle the option below that most accurately describes what sort of text it is.

website feature article letter persuasive text narrative

2 **Scan** the extract and list some of the presents that Dudley received for his birthday.

___

3 Scan the extract and use a highlighter to mark the parts in the passage that describe Harry's appearance.

4 Scan the extract and circle below the only physical characteristic that Harry likes about himself.

eyes scar hair legs face

skim Reading quickly, selecting key words and details through a text to determine the general meaning or main messages or ideas
scan To read, moving eyes quickly down a page, seeking specific words and phrases. It is also used when a reader first finds information to determine whether it will answer their questions

Comprehension focus 2: activating prior knowledge, connecting and questioning

The following text is an edited reproduction of an online recipe for raspberry chocolate swirl that appeared on the *Frankie* magazine website.

Scan the QR code or click here to access the Ingredients and Method.

RASPBERRY CHOCOLATE SWIRL

by Katherine Sabbath

Aside from eating the good stuff straight from out of the packet, this has always been my favourite thing to do with chocolate! Here's an easy-peasy recipe with little effort and a beautiful reward.
For baking beginners, there is no whisking, piping, rolling or fiddly bits. Just lots of creative and unbridled fun with chocolate and gorgeous raspberries. Melt it down, spread it out, swirl it around, add some tasty morsels and ... Ta-da!

While these make delicious treats on their own, they can also be used as fancy adornments to your cakes and desserts, as well as sweet gifts for friends.

11.2

Activity

1 This recipe is a procedural text. This means that it provides a procedure – a sequence of steps or instructions – to tell a reader how to make or do something. Circle other types of procedural texts from the list below.

short story   instruction manual   science experiment steps

novel   GPS route

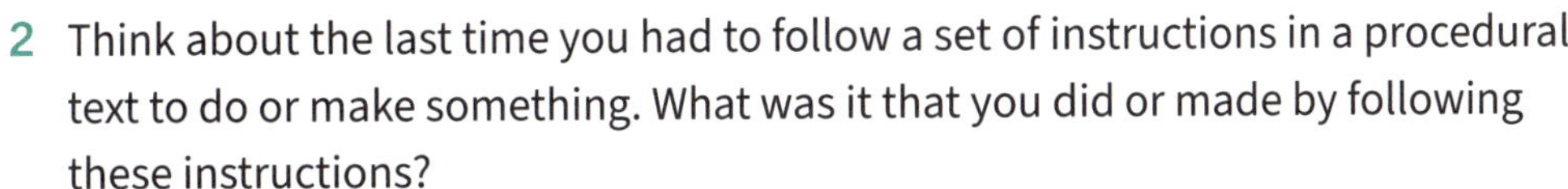

2 Think about the last time you had to follow a set of instructions in a procedural text to do or make something. What was it that you did or made by following these instructions?

____

3 How helpful were the instructions? Give reasons for your answer.

____

____

4 Look at the structure of the recipe. Why do you think a picture of the finished recipe is placed at the start?

____

5 Why are the ingredients listed before the instructions?

____

6 Why are the instructions numbered?

____

7 Why are there photographs alongside the instructions?

____

8 Does the language in the recipe make it appear easy or difficult to make the raspberry chocolate swirl? Give two short examples from the recipe to support your answer.

____

____

9 What is your favourite meal to eat? Find a recipe online that provides the steps for making this dish, and complete the table below.

Question	Answer
How many steps are in the online recipe you found?	
Does the recipe contain pictures?	
Is the recipe you found easier or harder to follow than the example provided for raspberry chocolate swirl? Explain why.	

Comprehension focus 3: scanning, skimming and summarising

11.3

Activity

Visit the *Earth Hour* website at earthhour.org.au

1 What is the first thing you notice when you open the home page? Explain why this feature captures your attention.

____

____

2 Make a list of the website features that help you navigate the site. These might include a navigation bar, indexes, menus, links or a site map.

____

____

3 Find a page on this website that includes background information about Earth Hour and write down where and when the organisation started.

____

____

4 Using only one sentence, summarise the main aim of Earth Hour.

____

____

Comprehension focus 4: scanning, visualising and inferring

The following extract is from a novel titled *The Bridge* written by New Zealand author Jane Higgins.

As soon as we stepped through the bridge gate into Southside, I knew that what we were trying to do was insane. You forget, sitting back home behind the high walls and the locked bridges—you forget that Southside is nearly half of a whole city, and the dark half at that. We gripped hands and I glanced at Fyffe. She looked filthy and fierce, every bit the hardened scavenger she wasn't.

We stepped off the bridge onto what must have been a major trucking route once. Maybe it used to be busy with warehouses and truckstop cafes and markets and storage halls. None of that was left. Now a packed dirt road stretched ahead of us, lined with a jumble of low shacks crammed together, rigged from fragments of the original Southside. They'd used chunks of concrete for foundations and sheets of iron for walls and roofs; planks of wood leaned over doorways, and ramshackle brick chimneys leaked smoke.

For all that it looked like a dump, though, it was humming. Different from the stony silence of the city after dark. This place was alive and peopled: dogs barked and kids yelled and charged about, and people criss-crossed the road ahead of us, talking, calling to each other, laughing and arguing. Some of them were lighting lamps and hanging them from the roofs of their makeshift shelters; others were building fires on grates by the roadside and huddling round them, warming themselves and cooking. Yes, cooking. The air just about knocked me over with the smell of spices and cooking oil and frying food.

11.4

Activity

1 Highlight the sensory descriptions in the excerpt using three different colours. For example, you could use:

- yellow for sight (visual **imagery**)
- pink for sound (auditory imagery)
- green for smell (olfactory imagery).

imagery Visually descriptive or figurative language to represent things including objects, actions and ideas in ways that appeal to the senses of the reader or viewer

2 Imagine what the setting looks like, sounds like and feels like. Decide on two **adjectives** that describe its atmosphere or appearance. Find supporting evidence from the passage.

Adjective	Evidence from the passage

3 Circle the option below that you think best describes how the narrator of *The Bridge* feels about arriving in Southside.

nervous but curious   terrified and hungry   excited and confident

4 What clues or evidence led you to infer this?

____

____

adjective A word class that describes, identifies or quantifies a noun or a pronoun, e.g. two (number or quantity), my (possessive), ancient (descriptive), shorter (comparative), wooden (classifying)

Comprehension focus 5: inferring, predicting and visualising

The following image is from an autobiographical graphic novel titled *Kampung Boy* by Lat (Mohammad Nor Khalid). *Kampung Boy* is about the author growing up in the 1950s in his village, a *kampung*, in rural Malaysia.

11.5

Activity

1 Look closely at the image and written caption in the reproduction above. Using the visual and written clues in the text, complete the table below by inferring the meanings of these features. Some parts of the table have been filled in to help you.

Clue	Mode of clue	Inferred meaning
Lat's family all gather to say goodbye to him.	visual	Lat comes from a loving family.
Friends of Lat's (the Meor brothers) also come to see him off.	visual and written	
		Lat's father cares about his son's comfort and happiness.
Lat says he is 'looking forward' to his new life.	written	
Lat and his father will travel by bicycle.		

2 What event do you **predict** will follow this part of the graphic novel extract?

____

____

3 Sketch the next frame of the graphic novel based on your prediction.

predicting An informed presumption about something that might happen. Predicting at the text level can include working out what a text might contain based on previous knowledge of the type of text

Comprehension focus 6: connecting, questioning and inferring

The formal letter below, which a father wrote to his six-year-old son, was posted online, where it went 'viral'.

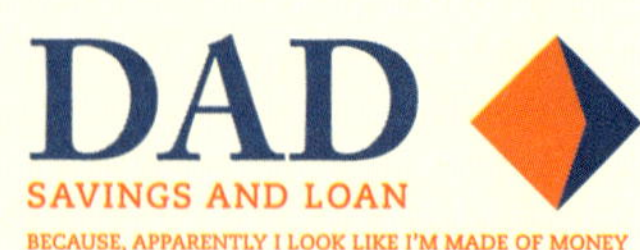

Dear [child's name]

We regret to inform you at this time that we are unable to provide a loan in the amount requested of $20.00. After reviewing your account, we have found you have insufficient funds, and a history of not doing your chores.

Furthermore, over $80.00 has been spent on discretionary entertainment expenses since Christmas. This is an unsustainable amount of expenditure, and we cannot further compound the problem by financially assisting with incurring further debt at this point.

If you would like to refute this decision, you can contact our complaint department at (Mom's number). Our dispute manager at this number may be able to persuade us to reverse our decision.

Thank you for choosing DAD Savings and Loan, we appreciate the chance to serve your financial needs.

Sincerely,

Dad
CEO, DAD S&L

11.6 Activity

1 What does it mean for something to go 'viral' online?

___

___

2 Can you think of any other texts, such as memes or videos, that have gone viral online? Record them below.

___

___

Comprehension focus 7: summarising and inferring

Australian artist Frederick McCubbin painted *The Pioneer* (below) in 1904. The painting is a triptych, a three-panelled painting. Each panel depicts an important moment in a visual story.

11.7

Activity

1 Look at each panel carefully, thinking about how each one works with the others to tell an overall story about the subjects (people). Summarise what you think is happening in each panel.

» Panel 1

____

____

» Panel 2

____

____

» Panel 3

____

____

2 Complete the following table with the evidence that led to you inferring the meanings of each panel in your answers above. Some parts of the table have been filled in to help you.

Visual features	Panel 1	Panel 2	Panel 3
Body language	Single female subject sits alone, gazing upwards.		
Setting		Some trees in the Australian bushland background have now been cleared.	
Symbolism			The cross that the male subject crouches near symbolises a grave.

visual features Visual components of a text which may include placement, salience, framing, representation of action or reaction, shot size, social distance and camera angle
symbolism The use of one object, person or situation to signify or represent another, by giving them meanings that are different from their literal sense (e.g. a dove is a symbol of peace)

Comprehension focus 8: activating prior knowledge, connecting and inferring

The following text is a poem written by Naomi Shihab Nye.

Valentine for Ernest Mann

You can't order a poem like you order a taco.
Walk up to the counter, say, 'I'll take two'
and expect it to be handed back to you
on a shiny plate.

Still, I like your spirit.
Anyone who says, 'Here's my address,
write me a poem,' deserves something in reply.
So I'll tell a secret instead:
poems hide. In the bottoms of our shoes,
they are sleeping. They are the shadows
drifting across our ceilings the moment

before we wake up. What we have to do
is live in a way that lets us find them.

Once I knew a man who gave his wife
two skunks for a valentine.
He couldn't understand why she was crying.
'I thought they had such beautiful eyes.'
And he was serious. He was a serious man
who lived in a serious way. Nothing was ugly
just because the world said so. He really
liked those skunks. So, he re-invented them
as valentines and they became beautiful.
At least, to him. And the poems that had been hiding
in the eyes of skunks for centuries
crawled out and curled up at his feet.

Maybe if we re-invent whatever our lives give us
we find poems. Check your garage, the odd sock
in your drawer, the person you almost like, but not quite.
And let me know.

11.8

Activity

1 What is your prior experience with poetry? List some of the poems you have read before. Think of childhood rhymes or songs if your prior experience of poetry is limited.

____

____

____

____

____

2 Brainstorm a list of features that you expect in a poem.

____

____

____

____

____

3 Did the text meet your expectations of a poem based on the features you listed for question 2?

---

4 What features of this text tell you that it is a poem and not a different form of writing, such as an article or a recipe?

---

5 What do you think is the main message of the poem? Explain your answer with evidence from the poem.

Comprehension focus 9: skimming, connecting and summarising

The following text is an extract from an online article written by Jo Cutler and Robin Banerjee. It was published on *The Conversation* website in 2018.

Five reasons why being kind makes you feel good – according to science

Everybody can appreciate acts of kindness. But when it comes to explaining why we do them, people often take one of two extreme positions. Some think kindness is something completely selfless that we do out of love and care, while others believe it is just a tool that we cunningly use to become more popular and reap the benefits.

But research shows that being kind to others can actually make us genuinely happy in a number of different ways. We know that deciding to be generous or cooperating with others activates an area of the brain called the striatum…The feel-good emotion from helping has been termed 'warm glow' and the activity we see in the striatum is the likely biological basis of that feeling.

… But why and how does kindness make us so happy? There are a number of different mechanisms involved, and how powerful they are in making us feel good may depend on our personalities.

1. Contagious smiling

Being kind is likely to make someone smile and if you see that smile for yourself, it might be catchy. A key theory about how we understand other people in neuroscience suggests that seeing someone else show an emotion automatically activates the same areas of the brain as if we experienced that emotion for ourselves ...

2. Righting a wrong

The same mechanism also makes us empathise with others when they are feeling negative, which could make us feel down. This is particularly true for close friends and family, as our representations of them in the brain physically overlap with our representations of ourselves. Doing a kind act to make someone who is sad feel better can also make us feel good – partly because we feel the same relief they do and partly because we are putting something right ...

3. Making connections

Being kind opens up many different possibilities to start or develop a social connection with someone. Kind acts such as buying someone a thoughtful present or even just a coffee strengthens friendships, and that in itself is linked to improved mood ...

4. A kind identity

Most people would like to think of themselves as a kind person, so acts of kindness help us to demonstrate that positive identity and make us feel proud of ourselves. In one recent study, even children in their first year of secondary school recognised how being kind can make you feel 'better as a person ... more complete', leading to feelings of happiness. This effect is even more powerful when the kind act links with other aspects of our personality, perhaps creating a more purposeful feeling ...

5. Kindness comes back around

Work on the psychology of kindness shows that one out of several possible motivations is reciprocity, the returning of a favour. This can happen directly or indirectly. Someone might remember that you helped them out last time and therefore be more likely to help you in the future. It could also be that one person being kind makes others in the group more kind, which lifts everyone's spirits ...

11.9

Activity

1 What are five reasons why kindness can make you feel good? The first example is provided.

	In the authors' words	Summarise in your own words
Reason 1	'Contagious smiling'	Kindness to others can make them smile and other people then copy that reaction and feel happy too.
Reason 2		
Reason 3		
Reason 4		
Reason 5		

2 Think of a time when you were kind to someone else. Did you experience the same benefits the authors describe in the article? Highlight your answer: Yes/No

3 Think about the benefits you did experience when you were kind to someone else (see question 2). Explain how they were similar to or different from the benefits described in the article.

______

______

______

4 This article was published in 2018. What important events have happened in the world since that time that have made the need for kindness to others even more important?

______

______

______

Comprehension focus 10: questioning, predicting and connecting

A great comprehension strategy is to ask ourselves questions before we start reading something, during the reading process and after we have finished reading.

The extract in the following activity is from a piece of writing titled 'Never Needed Fixing' by Eliza Hull. It was published in the *Growing Up Disabled in Australia* anthology (2021), a collection of autobiographical writing by more than 40 writers with disabilities or chronic illnesses.

11.10

Activity

1 Write down one pre-reading question you have about the text based on this description of it and its title. It could be about a clue or prediction based on the title that you want to know more about.

____

____

> I didn't grow up disabled; I grew up with a problem. A problem that those around me wanted to fix, and that I began to want to fix too.
>
> I was raised in Wodonga, a regional town 300 kilometres north-east of Melbourne. When I was five years old, I started falling over at school. I can still vividly recall the feeling of the rocks that got caught in my knees, the warm blood that would drip down my leg, and the numb, tingling sensation. My knees grew strong and firm.

2 Now write down another question you have part-way through the reading of this extract. It could be about something you are curious about or that interested you.

____

____

> There were doctor's appointments, hospital visits, questions and confusion, but never any answers. After each surgery, I watched red blood seep through my plaster casts, the hospital fairy would blow bubbles while I lay there, and celebrity footballers visited. Medical staff constantly talked about me, not to me. At five, I also started singing, which was a form of escape.
>
> After consulting with many specialists, my parents decided it was best for me to have several surgical procedures during my childhood. Their intention was to alleviate my symptoms and make my life easier. On reflection, as an adult, I understand that this is what every parent wants. They cared so much and tried as hard as they could. It must have been scary for them – the uncertainty of what life would be like for me – because difference is something most of us are taught to fear.

Improving your writing

This unit targets the knowledge and skills that will help improve the quality of your writing. Each activity is designed to help you revise or learn about a particular **language feature** or grammar **convention**. Understanding the different parts of speech – such as nouns, verbs, adjectives and so on – will enable you to communicate clearly with readers. There are lots of opportunities for you to apply your understanding of literacy and language in the writing activities of this unit. You will also be given prompts to practise editing sample sentences and paragraphs.

language features Features that support meaning (e.g. clause- and word-level grammar, vocabulary, figurative language, punctuation, images). Choices vary for the purpose, subject matter, audience and mode or medium

convention An accepted practice that has developed over time and is generally used and understood (e.g. use of punctuation)

Curriculum content

Australian Curriculum content description	Content code
Understand how complex and compound-complex sentences can be used to elaborate, extend and explain ideas.	AC9E7LA05
Understand how consistency of tense through verbs and verb groups achieves clarity in sentences.	AC9E7LA06
Understand the use of punctuation including colons and brackets to support meaning.	AC9E7LA09
Plan, create, edit and publish written and multimodal texts, selecting subject matter, and using text structures, language features, literary devices and visual features as appropriate to convey information, ideas and opinions in ways that may be imaginative, reflective, informative, persuasive and/or analytical.	AC9E7LY06
Understand how to use spelling rules and word origins; for example, Greek and Latin roots, base words, suffixes, prefixes and spelling patterns to learn new words and how to spell them.	AC9E7LY08

Nouns

Nouns are naming words. Nouns name objects, people, places, groups and emotions. There are five types of nouns.

Type of noun	What it names	Examples
common	ordinary things	boy, school, book
proper	particular things, including people and places	Harry, Hogwarts, London
collective	groups of things	flock (group of birds) class (group of students) bunch (group of bananas)
concrete	physical things you can see, touch, smell, hear or taste	laptop, stench, bottle
abstract	ideas, qualities and emotions that cannot be seen or touched	love, confidence, loyalty

noun A word class that includes all words denoting person, place, object or thing, idea or emotion. Nouns may be common, proper, collective, abstract and compound

12.1

Activity

1 Fill in each gap in the table with an appropriate common noun or proper noun.

Common noun	Proper noun
	Granny Smith
city	
	Mount Kosciuszko
car	

2 Choose the correct collective noun to complete each phrase below.

school murder parliament library pack

a ______________________ of cards

b ______________________ of books

c ______________________ of fish

d ______________________ of crows

e ______________________ of owls

3 Circle the abstract noun in each sentence. (Some sentences may contain more than one.)

a He was in a very good mood until lunchtime.

b Fear made his hair stand on end.

c She had a funny feeling she'd had the same dream before.

d They both sensed the danger that lurked nearby.

e His positivity was clear to everyone who met him.

Adjectives

Adjectives describe or modify nouns by giving additional information about them. For example:

» Spot is an adorable dog.

» The film is innovative and exciting.

Adjectives provide 'colour' to a piece of writing. They help to make characters and settings come to life by creating pictures in the minds of readers. They also help to make the description more precise and specific.

adjective A word class that describes, identifies or quantifies a noun or a pronoun, e.g. two (number or quantity), my (possessive), ancient (descriptive), shorter (comparative), wooden (classifying)

12.2

Activity

1 Use a thesaurus to find more interesting adjectives for the following descriptions of a film or book. The first one has been done for you as an example.

a good satisfying, wonderful, engaging

b bad ______________________________

c funny ______________________________

d scary ______________________________

e sad ______________________________

Comparative and superlative adjectives

Adjectives of degree compare the qualities of people or things. They include *comparative* and *superlative* adjectives.

Comparative adjectives are used to compare the qualities of two things or people. Some examples are:

» My brother is taller than me, but I am older than him.

» The teachers get to school earlier than the students.

» I think the beach is more beautiful than the city.

Superlative adjectives are used to compare three or more things. They show the highest degree of difference compared with the other things. Some examples are:

» Of the three sisters, Khloe is the tallest, Kourtney is the strongest and Kylie is the youngest.

» The Prime Minister is the most powerful person in Australia.

Sometimes we add the suffixes '–er' or '–est' to show comparative and superlative degrees, as in the following example: young, young*er* and young*est*.

12.3

Activity

1 Tick the sentences below that use comparative or superlative adjectives correctly.

a Today is hottest than yesterday. ☐

b If you win the lottery, you are the luckiest person in the world. ☐

c This kitten is the smaller one in the litter of five. ☐

d She was the tallest of all her sisters. ☐

e He was the faster runner of his whole school. ☐

2 Fill in each of the gaps below with the correct comparative or superlative form of the adjective in brackets.

a Of all the dogs in the shelter, the labradoodle had the ____________ hair. (curly)

b My grandpa is ____________ than my grandma by two months. (old)

c The film festival is showing the ____________ films in history. (famous)

d When we lost the grand final, I was upset, my captain was ____________ than me, but our coach was ____________ of everyone. (upset)

e The tree they chose for their cubby house was the ____________ in their backyard. (tall)

Verbs

verb A word class that expresses processes that include doing, feeling, thinking, saying and relating
verb group Consists of a main verb, alone or preceded by one or more auxiliary or modal verbs as modifiers
pronoun A word that takes the place of a noun (e.g. I, me, he, she, herself, you, it, that, they, few, many, who, whoever, someone, everybody, and many others)

A **verb** describes doing, being or having. A verb can be made up of one word or more than one word (a **verb group**). Without a verb of some kind, a sentence is not grammatically correct.

Noun-verb agreement

A verb has to match the noun/**pronoun** or number in the sentence. This is called noun–verb agreement.

Noun/pronoun: a verb has to match the form of the noun or pronoun (person) in the sentence. The table below shows the forms of the verb 'to love' in relation to the pronouns used.

Pronoun	Form	Example
first (I)	love	I love chocolate.
second (you)	love	You love chocolate.
third (he/she/it)	loves	She loves chocolate.

Number: a verb also has to match the number of the noun or pronoun (person) in the sentence. If the noun is singular, the verb must also be singular. If the noun is plural, the verb must also be in the correct plural form. The table below shows the singular and plural forms of the verb 'to be'.

Singular	Plural	Example
I am	we are	I am wet.
you are	you [all] are	You are wet.
he is/she is/it is	they are	They are wet.

Verb-tense agreement

A verb form must also match the tense of the sentence. This is called verb–tense agreement. **Tense** tells us when the action occurred. The three main tenses are past, present and future. The table below shows the forms of the verbs 'to be' and 'to talk'.

Verb	Past	Present	Future
to be	I was happy.	I am happy.	I will be happy.
to talk	I talked/I was talking.	I talk/I am talking.	I will talk/I will be talking.

tense The form a verb takes to signal the location of a clause in time (e.g. present tense 'has' in 'Jo has a cat' locates the situation in the present; past tense 'had' in 'Jo had a cat' locates it in the past)

12.4

Activity

1 Rewrite each sentence below so that the verb agrees with the person and number, making it a grammatically correct sentence.

a Kat ride her bike to school.

____

b Mum and Dad wants me to learn the piano.

____

c I needs a great summer holiday.

____

2 Which word correctly completes the sentence below?

The first time I flew in a plane I am/are/was ______________ ten years old.

3 Fill in the gaps in each sentence below with the appropriate tense of the verb in brackets.

a When the accident happened, Amelia (call) ______________ the ambulance.

b If it (snow) ______________ this week, we (ski) ______________ in the alps.

c Shhh! The baby (sleep) ______________

4 Circle the correct form of the verb in each sentence below.

a One of my friends is/are in a bad mood today.

b Oil and water do/does not mix.

c My brother and I was/were good at tennis when we were younger.

Imperative verbs

Imperative verbs give orders or instructions. They are the verbs you would use if you were bossing someone around. Examples include:

» Give me that!

» Clean your room.

» Beat the eggs, then add the milk.

imperative verb A verb that gives an order or instruction (e.g. 'Open the door')

12.5

Activity

1 Change the following sentences into imperative commands.

a I wish you would walk the dog after school.

____

b You might like to take off your shoes before you come inside.

____

2 The thoughtful choice of verbs can help to make your writing more interesting and precise. Replace the following verbs with more specific ones to make the sentences more interesting.

a Sam jumped ______________ for joy when she found out she had won first prize.

b They walked ______________ slowly up the beach while the sun set on the horizon.

c He ran ______________ as fast as his legs could carry him.

d She looked ______________ at him carefully, trying to work out where she knew him from.

e We went ______________ to the beach once the sun came out.

Adverbs

Adverbs describe or add meaning to verbs, adjectives and other adverbs. There are four different types of adverbs.

Type of adverb	What it describes	Example
adverb of manner	how	She walked quickly.
adverb of time	when	I'll do it tomorrow.
adverb of place	where	He left his wallet there.
adverb of degree	how much, how little, how likely	The water was extremely cold.

adverb A word class that may modify a verb (e.g. 'softly' in 'the boy sings softly'), an adjective (e.g. 'really' in 'he is really strong') or another adverb (e.g. 'very' in 'the toddler walks very slowly')

Sometimes it's easy to recognise an adverb because it ends with 'ly', but this is not always the case. Not all adverbs end in 'ly', and not all words that end in 'ly' are adverbs!

12.6

Activity

1 Place the adverbs from the list below into the correct columns of the table that follows. An example of each has been provided for you.

before	quite	easily	there
now	soon	everywhere	quickly
almost	badly	rather	away
carefully	here	very	then

Adverb of manner	Adverb of time	Adverb of place	Adverb of degree
easily	now	everywhere	quite

2 Adverbs are often formed by adding –ly to an adjective. (Sometimes a slight spelling change needs to be made to the adjective to form an adverb.) Some examples are:

» loud → loudly (The trumpeter played loudly.)

» hungry → hungrily (The dog whined hungrily.)

3 Form adverbs from the adjectives below.

a happy ______

b lucky ______

c necessary ______

d probable ______

e accidental ______

4 Write *one* sentence that includes any *two* of the adverbs you have formed in your answer above.

______

______

Prepositions

A **preposition** is a word that describes the relationship between words in a sentence. For example:

- The book is on my desk.
- I will clean up after lunch.

The noun that follows the preposition is called the 'object' of that preposition. To find the object, always ask *who* or *what* after the preposition. For example:

preposition A word class that usually describes the relationship between words in a sentence. Prepositions can indicate: space (e.g. 'on'), time (e.g. 'after') and other relationships (e.g. 'of', 'except')

prepositional phrase A group of words that typically consists of a preposition followed by a noun group/phrase (e.g. 'on the train' in 'we met on the train'; 'on golf' in 'keen on golf')

- The book is on my desk. 'On what?' My desk. 'My desk' is the object of the preposition 'on'.
- I will clean up after lunch. 'After what?' Lunch. 'Lunch' is the object of the preposition 'after'.

The preposition and its object together are called a **prepositional phrase**. The following are prepositional phrases:

- 'on my desk'
- 'after lunch'.

Prepositions can indicate space and time.

Type of preposition	Common prepositions	Examples
space	above, below, near, to, from, on, under, between, beside, inside, outside, over, through	She's in the garden, under the tree.
time	before, after, during, now, then, on, at, in	He's available on Friday, before noon.

12.7 Activity

1 Circle the prepositions and underline the prepositional phrases in the following sentences.

a The moon revolves around the Earth.

b I love to get up before sunrise.

c My friends and I catch the bus to school.

d Let's get laksa from the Malaysian restaurant.

e He came home late from the party.

2 Complete the following expressions with the correct preposition.

a to be angry ______________________ someone

b to compare something ______________________ something else

c to rely ______________________ someone

d to arrive ______________________ a place

e to stick ______________________ a friend

Conjunctions

A **conjunction** acts as a *joining* word. It can join words, phrases or sentences. Look at these examples:

» The girl was young but reliable.
» It was cold and wet.
» We felt hungry as we'd had no chance to eat yet.

conjunction In a sentence, a word that joins other words, groups/ phrases or clauses together in a logical relationship such as addition, time, cause or comparison. There are 2 types: coordinating and subordinating

A conjunction can also show *relationships* between **phrases** and **clauses**, acting like an adverb and telling us the *when*, *where*, *why* and the *order* of events. Look closely at these examples:

» We have been friends since kindergarten. (tells *when*)
» My dog wants to come with me wherever I go. (tells *where*)
» The baby cried because it was hungry. (tells *why*)
» I always brush my teeth after dinner. (tells the *order* of events)

phrase A group of words often beginning with a preposition but without a subject and verb combination (e.g. 'on the river'; 'with brown eyes')
clause A grammatical unit referring to a happening or state e.g. 'the team won' (happening), 'the dog is red' (state), usually containing a subject and a verb group/ phrase

Common conjunctions

and	but	or	so	when
while	than	then	where	since
because	as	for	unless	if
after	until	although	yet	

12.8 Activity

1 Circle the conjunction in each sentence below.

a Playing soccer makes me feel tired but happy.
b Close the door before getting changed.
c I hid the lollies where my brother won't find them.
d Try to cheer her up since she is sad today.
e I dunk the tea bag in the hot water then add the milk.

2 Join each of these pairs of sentences into one sentence by using an appropriate conjunction. Some changes in wording may be necessary.

a The neighbours moved house. They had a baby.

____

b I'm not allowed to watch TV. I finish my homework.

____

c This is the laundry. My cat sleeps in the laundry.

____

Prefixes

A **prefix** is added to the beginning of a word to change its meaning. The original word is called the '**base word**'. For example, in 'disagree', *dis* is the prefix and *agree* is the base.

prefix A meaningful element (morphemes) added to the beginning of a word to change its meaning (e.g. 'un' to 'happy' to make 'unhappy')
base word A form of a word that conveys the essential meaning. It is not derived from or made up of other words and has no prefixes or suffixes (e.g. action, activate, react are all from the base word 'act')

Prefixes change the meaning of the base word. In this example, the prefix 'dis–' changes the base word 'agree', so to 'disagree' means to 'not agree'. Prefixes usually have Latin or Greek origins and have their own meaning, but a prefix cannot be a word on its own. 'Pre–' comes from the Latin for 'before'.

12.9 Activity

1 Circle the prefixes in the following words:

semicircle uninterested expel disinherit
misleading supernatural impolite

2 Modern English can invent new prefixes to create new words. Complete the table below.

Prefix	Meaning	Examples
franken–	From *Frankenstein* – i.e. something that becomes terrifying to its maker	frankenfood (genetically modified food), frankenfish, frankenfarm
e–		
cyber–		

3 For each of the following prefixes, provide two examples of words that use that prefix. Use a dictionary if you need help.

Prefix	Meaning	Examples
anti–	against	antibiotics, antisocial
auto–	self	
bi–	two, twice	
co–/com–/con–	together, with	
contra–	against	

Prefix	Meaning	Examples
de–	down, from, away	
fore–	before, in front of	
non–	not	

Suffixes

Suffixes like prefixes, are added to a word, except they are placed at the *ends* of base words. A suffix adds meaning to a word, and knowing suffixes will increase your vocabulary.

suffix An element added to the end of a word to change its meaning (e.g. to form past tense: '-ed'; to show a smaller amount or degree: -less; to form an adverb: -ly)

The addition of a suffix often requires the spelling of the base word to be changed slightly. For example, in the word 'suffocation', *suffocate* is the base and *–ion* is the suffix.

12.10

Activity

1 Fill in the gaps in the table below.

Suffix	Makes	Meaning	Example
–er/–or	noun	person who does	teacher, inventor
–	noun	position, state or skill of	friendship, leadership
ian	noun		guardian, electrician
–	verb	make or become	terrify, falsify
–ate	verb	make or become	
–able/–ible	adjective	capable of being	
–ful	adjective		beautiful, spiteful
–less	adjective	without	
–wise/–ward	adverb		clockwise, backward
–ly	adverb	in that way	

1 Match the causes to their effects below.

Cause	Effect
teens not getting enough sleep	may result in less physical activity and children being more disengaged or less attentive, and may negatively affect family functioning
high levels of chemicals (CFCs) polluting the atmosphere	impacting their mental wellbeing, increasing their risk of depression, anxiety and low self-esteem
children spend too much time in front of screens	the ozone layer is depleting

Connectives can also be used to transition smoothly between one point, sentence or paragraph and the next. They create **cohesion** in your writing. Read the examples below.

in addition	moreover	additionally	also
however	by contrast	soon	on the other hand
in summary	overall	finally	on the whole
previously			

2 Which of the words or phrases above might be suitable to start the following parts of a piece of writing? (There may be more than one correct option.)

a a second or third body paragraph in a persuasive essay ______________________

b a conclusion in an analytical essay ______________________

c an opposing argument in a persuasive text ______________________

3 Create a short persuasive paragraph in response to the topic 'winter is better than summer'. Make sure to use connectives to transition between points or sentences.

____

____

____

____

____

cohesion Grammatical or lexical relationships that bind different parts of a text together and give it unity. It is achieved through devices such as reference, substitution, repetition and text connectives

Complex sentences

A **complex sentence** has a main piece of information (which could be a simple sentence on its own) called the 'main clause' and some extra information (that could *not* be a sentence on its own) called the 'subordinate clause' which is joined with a **subordinating conjunction**. Adding extra information increases the density and complexity of a sentence.

complex sentence A sentence with one or more subordinate clauses. In the following example, the subordinate clause is shown in brackets: I took my umbrella [because it was raining]
subordinating conjunction Words that introduce clauses that add or extend information. They include conjunctions such as 'after', 'when', 'because', 'if' and 'that'

Main piece of information	Extra information
The snowboarder fell over	when she hit an icy patch.

The reason for including this extra information in the form of a subordinate clause is to highlight the cause (hitting an icy patch) of the effect or action (falling over). That is, we arrange clauses purposefully, not randomly.

If you include the main clause first, the sentence doesn't need a comma. For example:

» The snowboarder fell over when she hit an icy patch.

However, if you place the subordinate clause first, a comma is needed. For example:

» When she hit an icy patch, the snowboarder fell over.

12.12

Activity

1 Tick the complex sentences in the list below.

a They ordered fish and chips. ☐

b After a day at the beach, they ordered fish and chips. ☐

c They ordered fish and chips after a day at the beach. ☐

d Shimila, Chantel, Phoebe and I ordered fish and chips. ☐

2 Underline the main clause in these complex sentences.

a Don't talk about the ending of the TV series until I've seen it.

b When you've finished washing the dishes, I will help you dry them.

c She rides her bike to school because it's faster than walking.

d Even though Brock rang the doorbell three times, nobody answered.

e While moving quickly, he pushed through the crowded concert.

3 Make these sentences into complex sentences by adding a subordinate clause.

a ______________________________, I had breakfast.

b I went to the party ______________________________.

c ______________________________, I visited my grandma.

d Everyone was shocked ______________________________.

e She sat down ______________________________.

Semicolons and colons

semicolon Punctuation (;) used to join closely related clauses that could stand alone as sentences and can be used to separate long items in a list
colon Punctuation mark (:) that separates a general statement from one or more statements that give extra information, explanation or illustration. Statements after a colon do not have to be full sentences

Effective use of punctuation, such as **semicolons** and **colons**, can be used to support the meaning of a piece of writing.

Semicolons

A semicolon consists of a dot above a comma. It looks like this.

;

A semicolon has two purposes:

- to show a relationship between two main clauses in a sentence (a main clause is one that could be used as a sentence in its own right)
- to separate items in a list when the individual items already have commas in them.

Read the examples below.

- I wanted to get a burger; he wanted to have salad.
- It was a Greek salad with black pitted olives; amazing, crumbly fetta; ripe, juicy tomato; and crisp, green lettuce leaves fresh from the garden that morning.

Colons

A colon is two dots, one above the other. It looks like this.

:

A colon is used to mark off the main part of a sentence and introduce additional information, such as a list. A colon can also be used to separate the speaker from their dialogue in a play script. Read the examples below.

- Just remember four things: chocolate, apples, ice and an axe.
- Pai: In the old days, the land felt a great emptiness.

12.13 Activity

1 Insert semicolons in the correct places in the following sentences.

a Pai knew what would happen next she knew her Koro well.

b On the beach, she found three small, delicate bones a dead penguin, which had been decomposing since the storm and an old fishing basket.

c She wanted nothing more than to fulfil her destiny she just didn't know where to begin.

2 Cross out the colons that are incorrect in the following sentences.

a The coach: told them what they needed to do: to win: play hard: keep their eyes on the ball and never give up.

b Don't bring nuts: on camp: Amanda and Ellie are allergic to them.

c She had two options left to her: eat the pie: or stay hungry.

d The trip was a failure: for two reasons: poor planning and terrible accommodation.

e He was convinced: without a doubt: the bag had been stolen.

3 Punctuate the following short paragraphs correctly using semicolons, colons, commas and full stops. You may also need to change some letters to capital letters.

a The holiday was great it was sunny it never rained we all got along and there was so much to do I wish Alex had been there he is always such fun the life of the party

b I had forgotten how uncomfortable the house was water leaked through the roof floorboards creaked no door shut properly windows didn't close and there was a musty smell still we made our own fun it was the last time we were all together

c I completely agree we have so many amazing animals and plants kangaroos wombats koalas and gum trees

4 These sentences are all punctuated incorrectly. Rewrite them with the correct punctuation.

a I slept through my alarm this morning, I had to run for the bus.

____

b Three people are staying at my house; my grandma, my grandpa and my aunt.

____

c My cat always sleeps in the warmest spot, today it is on top of my laptop.

____

Brackets

Brackets, also called 'parentheses', can also be used to support meaning in writing. This form of punctuation is used to add information to a sentence. Brackets can enclose a word or phrase, but the sentence should still make sense without the information inside the brackets. Brackets can be used in the following situations.

Effect of including bracket	Example
clarifies meaning by adding extra but not essential information	I can't wait to go to Art (my favourite subject) tomorrow.
introduces an acronym or shortened title that is used in the rest of the text	I couldn't believe that National Aeronautics and Space Administration (NASA) actually replied to my letter!
indicates an aside that a character may be thinking	He slowly turned to face me (the butterflies in my stomach went crazy!) and I smiled shyly.

12.14 Activity

Place brackets where they belong in the sentences below.

1 The Royal Society for the Prevention of Cruelty to Animals RSPCA is an organisation that provides care to animals who have been mistreated.

2 Mum lectured me about the dangers of not getting sleep eye roll but I really wasn't listening.

3 The winner of the competition who had won it five times already was only 18 years old.

Focus on spelling

The 'i before e except after c' rule

Do you know the rule '*i* before *e* except after *c*'? It can be used to help you remember how to spell words that have *i* and *e* together.

Examples of words that follow the 'i before e except after c' rule are 'bel**ie**ve', 'p**ie**ce', 'th**ie**f', 'perc**ei**ve', '**cei**ling' and 're**cei**pt'.

However, some words break this rule, and you need to learn the exceptions.

Examples of words that break the 'i before e except after c' rule are 's**ei**ze', 'v**ei**n', 'for**ei**gn', 's**cie**nce', 'spe**cie**s' and 'gla**cie**r'.

12.15 Activity

1 Circle the correct spelling from each word pair:

a I'm inviting my freind/friend over for dinner.

b Sometimes our neighbour/nieghbour collects our mail.

c My brother is acting wierd/weird.

d It's nice to recieve/receive gifts on your birthday.

e My suitcase was over the weight/wieght limit.

2 Write *ie* or *ei* in the space to complete each word.

a rel________ ve

b n________ ce

c pr________ st

d ach________ ve

e f________ sty

f p________ rce

3 Circle the correct spelling of these frequently misspelled words.

a achieve/acheive

b soldier/soilder/solider

c definetley/definitely/definately

d embarrass/embarass

e arguement/argument

f tomorrow/tommorrow

4 Spellcheck software will sometimes autocorrect to American instead of Standard Australian English spellings. Sort the following words into their correct columns.

	American spelling	Standard Australian English spelling
favourite/favorite pyjamas/pajamas theatre/theater tire/tyre recognize/recognise		

Proofreading, editing and redrafting

It is very important that you carefully proofread and **edit** your writing to correct any mistakes. Often, you will need to redraft and change some of your writing to improve it. Below is a list of helpful tips to ensure that your writing is as good as it can be.

Proofreading, editing and redrafting checklist		
To check	**Action to take**	**Tick when complete**
Is everything you have written relevant to the task or topic? Does any content need to be cut out?	Eliminate any content that does not serve the **purpose** of the piece of writing.	
Is your writing well organised? Does it follow a logical order, consistent with the type of text you are writing?	Sometimes a piece of evidence is better suited to a different paragraph, so move your points and evidence if necessary.	
Does your writing include enough detail and/or explanation?	If your ideas are not properly developed, add more information or explanation. An imaginative piece of writing may need more vivid description, and an informative piece may need more detail.	

Scan the QR code or click here to access additional tips.

edit To prepare, alter, adapt or refine with attention to grammar, spelling, punctuation and vocabulary

purpose An intended or assumed reason for a type of text

Glossary

adjective A word class that describes, identifies or quantifies a noun or a pronoun, e.g. two (number or quantity), my (possessive), ancient (descriptive), shorter (comparative), wooden (classifying).

adverb A word class that may modify a verb (e.g. 'softly' in 'the boy sings softly'), an adjective (e.g. 'really' in 'he is really strong') or another adverb (e.g. 'very' in 'the toddler walks very slowly').

aesthetic Concerned with a sense of beauty or an appreciation of artistic expression.

alliteration A recurrence of the same consonant sounds at the beginning of words in close succession (e.g. 'ripe, red raspberry').

assonance The repetition of vowel sounds within words (e.g. rain, main).

attitudes Particular ways of thinking and feeling towards people or things.

audience An intended or assumed group of readers, listeners or viewers that a writer, designer, filmmaker or speaker is addressing.

base word A form of a word that conveys the essential meaning. It is not derived from or made up of other words and has no prefixes or suffixes (e.g. action, activate, react are all from the base word 'act').

cinematography The science and art of shooting motion-picture scenes, including the camera work and lighting.

clause A grammatical unit referring to a happening or state e.g. 'the team won' (happening), 'the dog is red' (state), usually containing a subject and a verb group/phrase.

cohesion Grammatical or lexical relationships that bind different parts of a text together and give it unity. It is achieved through devices such as reference, substitution, repetition and text connectives.

colon Punctuation mark (:) that separates a general statement from one or more statements that give extra information, explanation or illustration. Statements after a colon do not have to be full sentences.

complex sentence A sentence with one or more subordinate clauses. In the following example, the subordinate clause is shown in brackets: I took my umbrella [because it was raining].

compound sentence A sentence with 2 or more main clauses of equal grammatical status, usually marked by a coordinating conjunction, e.g. [Ira came home this morning] [but he didn't stay long].

comprehension strategies Processes used by readers to make meaning from texts. They include activating and using prior knowledge, predicting likely future events in a text, monitoring meaning and critically reflecting.

conjunction In a sentence, a word that joins other words, groups/phrases or clauses together in a logical relationship such as addition, time, cause or comparison. There are 2 types: coordinating and subordinating.

connective Words linking, and logically relating ideas to one another, in paragraphs and sentences indicating relationships of time, cause and effect, comparison, addition, condition and concession or clarification.

context An environment or situation (social, cultural or historical) in which a text is responded to or created. Or wording surrounding an unfamiliar word, which a reader or listener uses to understand its meaning.

contraction An abbreviated version of a word or words, often formed by shortening a word or merging 2 words into one (e.g. doctor: Dr; do not: don't).

convention An accepted practice that has developed over time and is generally used and understood (e.g. use of punctuation).

dialect Form of a language distinguished by features of vocabulary, grammar and pronunciation particular to a region.

edit To prepare, alter, adapt or refine with attention to grammar, spelling, punctuation and vocabulary.

evaluative language Positive or negative language that judges the worth of something. It includes language to express feelings and opinions; make judgements; and assess quality of objects, ideas and features of texts.

hybrid text A composite text resulting from a purposeful mixing of elements from different sources or genres (e.g. 'infotainment').

idiom An expression whose meaning does not relate to the literal meaning of its words (e.g. 'They went out to paint the town red').

imagery Visually descriptive or figurative language to represent things including objects, actions and ideas in ways that appeal to the senses of the reader or viewer.

imperative verb A verb that gives an order or instruction (e.g. 'open the door').

jargon Technical words specific to a certain group, such as medical or legal jargon.

language features Features that support meaning e.g. clause- and word-level grammar, vocabulary, figurative language, punctuation, images. Choices vary for the purpose, subject matter, audience and mode or medium.

literary text Past and contemporary texts across a range of cultural contexts which are valued for their form and style and are recognised as having artistic value.

metalanguage Vocabulary including technical terms, concepts, ideas or codes used to describe or discuss a language. The language of grammar and the language of literary criticism are examples.

metaphor A type of figurative language used to describe a person or object through an implicit comparison to something with similar characteristics.

mise en scène In film, the composition of a shot, including elements such as lighting, costumes, props, set design and special effects.

modal verb A verb that expresses a degree of probability attached by a speaker or writer to a statement (e.g. 'I might come home') or a degree of obligation (e.g. 'You must give it to me').

mode Various processes of communication – listening, speaking, reading or viewing and writing or creating.

multimodal A combination of 2 or more communication modes (e.g. print, image and spoken text, as in film or computer presentations).

narrative The selection and sequencing of events or experiences, real or imagined, to tell a story to entertain, engage, inform and extend imagination, typically using an orientation, complication and resolution.

noun A word class that includes all words denoting person, place, object or thing, idea or emotion. Nouns may be common, proper, collective, abstract and compound.

perspective A lens through which the author perceives the world and creates a text, or the lens through which the reader or viewer perceives the world and understands a text.

phrase A group of words often beginning with a preposition but without a subject and verb combination (e.g. 'on the river'; 'with brown eyes').

point of view The position from which the text is designed to be perceived (e.g. a narrator might take a role of first or third person, omniscient or restricted in knowledge of events or the opinion presented in a text)

predicting An informed presumption about something that might happen. Predicting at the text level can include working out what a text might contain based on previous knowledge of the type of text.

prefix A meaningful element (morphemes) added to the beginning of a word to change its meaning (e.g. 'un' to 'happy' to make 'unhappy').

preposition A word class that usually describes the relationship between words in a sentence. Prepositions can indicate space (e.g. 'on'), time (e.g. 'after') and other relationships (e.g. 'of', 'except').

prepositional phrase A group of words that typically consists of a preposition followed by a noun group/phrase (e.g. 'on the train' in 'we met on the train'; 'on golf' in 'keen on golf').

pronoun A word that takes the place of a noun (e.g. I, me, he, she, herself, you, it, that, they, few, many, who, whoever, someone, everybody, and many others).

protagonist The main character in a text.

purpose An intended or assumed reason for a type of text.

salience A strategy of emphasis, highlighting what is important in a text. In images, it is achieved through strategies such as the placement of an item in the foreground, size and contrast in tone or colour.

scan To read, moving one's eyes quickly down a page seeking specific words and phrases. It is also used when a reader first finds information to determine whether it will answer their questions.

semicolon Punctuation (;) used to join closely related clauses that could stand alone as sentences and can be used to separate long items in a list.

simile A device comparing 2 things that are not alike. Similes use 'like', 'as' or 'than' to make the comparison (e.g. The cake was as light as air).

skim Reading quickly, selecting key words and details through a text to determine the general meaning or main messages or ideas.

Standard Australian English Recognised as the 'common language' of Australians, it is the dynamic and evolving spoken and written English used for official or public purposes, and recorded in dictionaries, style guides and grammars.

stereotype An oversimplified idea about a person or group and believing that all people in that group are the same, e.g. a stereotype of women might assert that they are all gentle and caring, while a stereotype of men might assert that they can't share their feelings.

style The distinctive language features, text structures and/or subject matter in a text which may shape meaning, be enjoyed for its aesthetic qualities or distinguish the work of an author, period etc.

subject A word or group of words (usually a noun group/phrase) in a sentence or clause representing the person, thing or idea doing the action that follows (e.g. 'The dog [subject] was barking').

subject matter The topic or theme under consideration.

subordinating conjunction Words that introduce clauses that add or extend information. They include conjunctions such as 'after', 'when', 'because', 'if' and 'that'.

suffix An element added to the end of a word to change its meaning (e.g. to form past tense: '-ed'; to show a smaller amount or degree: -less; to form an adverb: -ly).

symbolism The use of one object, person or situation to signify or represent another by giving them meanings that are different from their literal sense (e.g. a dove is a symbol of peace).

synonym A word having nearly the same meaning as others (e.g. synonyms for 'old' include 'aged', 'venerable', 'antiquated').

tense The form a verb takes to signal the location of a clause in time (e.g. present tense 'has' in 'Jo has a cat' locates the situation in the present; past tense 'had' in 'Jo had a cat' locates it in the past).

theme The main idea, concept or message of a text.

tone The mood created by the language features used by an author and the way the text makes the reader feel.

values Ideas and beliefs specific to individuals and groups.

verb A word class that expresses processes that include doing, feeling, thinking, saying and relating.

verb group Consists of a main verb, alone or preceded by one or more auxiliary or modal verbs as modifiers.

visual features Visual components of a text which may include placement, salience, framing, representation of action or reaction, shot size, social distance and camera angle.

voice The distinct personality of a piece of writing; the individual writing style of the composer, created through the way they use and mix various language features (e.g. a narrative using a child's voice).

Acknowledgements

Insight Publications thanks the following writers for their contributions *to Australian Curriculum English Year 7*: Leanne Bondin and Adam Kealley.

Insight Publications is also grateful to the following individuals and organisations for permission to reproduce copyright material.

Texts: Extract from *Catch a Falling Star - Things That Fall From the Sky* by Meg McKinlay, Walker Books, 2019; Extract from *Young Dark Emu: A Truer History* by Bruce Pascoe, Magabala Books, (Broome, 2019); 'Fast-food giants and TikTok build base of child brand ambassadors' by Susie O'Brien, Kids News, 2022; Extract from *Freedom from Fear* Australia Day Address, © Deng Thiak Adut, 2016; *Extract from Different, Not Less: A neurodivergent's guide to embracing your true self and finding your happily ever after* by Chloé Hayden, Murdoch Books, 2022; 'Face of the City' by Grace Perry, *The ABC Book of Australian Poetry: A treasury of poems for young people* compiled by Libby Hathorn, ABC Books, 2010*;* 'In the Forest' by Thomas Shapcott in *The Mankind Thing*, Jacaranda Press, 1964; Extract from *Run* by Tim Sinclair, Penguin, 2013; Extracts from: *Runt* by Craig Silvey, Allen & Unwin, 2022; 'Book Club: Runt is Craig Silvey's first young readers book following on from Jasper Jones and Honeybee' by Gemma Nisbet, The West Australian, 2022; Extract from *Harry Potter and the Philosopher's Stone* © J.K. Rowling, 1997, reproduced with permission from The Blair Partnership; Extract from *The Bridge* © Jane Higgins, 2011, reproduced with permission from The Text Publishing Company Pty Ltd; 'Valentine for Ernest Mann', by Naomi Shihab Nye in Red Suitcase, BOA Editions, 1994; 'Five reasons why being kind makes you feel good – according to science' by Jo Cutler, and Robin Banerjee University of Sussex, *The Conversation, 2018*; 'Never Needed Fixing' by Eliza Hull in *Growing Up Disabled in Australi*a edited by Carly Findlay. Black Inc, 2021; 'Raspberry Chocolate Swirl' recipe reproduced with permission from Katherine Sabbath© 2016 Katherine Sabbath, All Rights Reserved.

Images: Allen & Unwin, covers of *Tiger Daughter*, *How to Bee* and *Runt*; Colour image of *UP* movie poster from Alamy; 3 Coloured Posters from WWF: Earth Hour wifi, Earth Hour lightbulb, Earth hour forest; Three screenshots from Dreaming story of the Butu Wugun (Black Crow) and Wibung (Magpie), voiced by Paul Teerman and animated by Jaime Aguilar (@GuavaJagular), produced by CuriousWorks as part of the 2020 NAIDOC Week program CREDIT Jaime Aguilar (@GuavaJagular) as the animator and CuriousWorks for producing and created by Liverpool Council and Casula Powerhouse; *Kampung Boy* by Lat (Mohammad Nor Khalid); *The Pioneer* (oil on canvas) © Frederick McCubbin, 1904, reproduced with permission from the National Gallery of Victoria. Additional images from Shutterstock.